I0752492

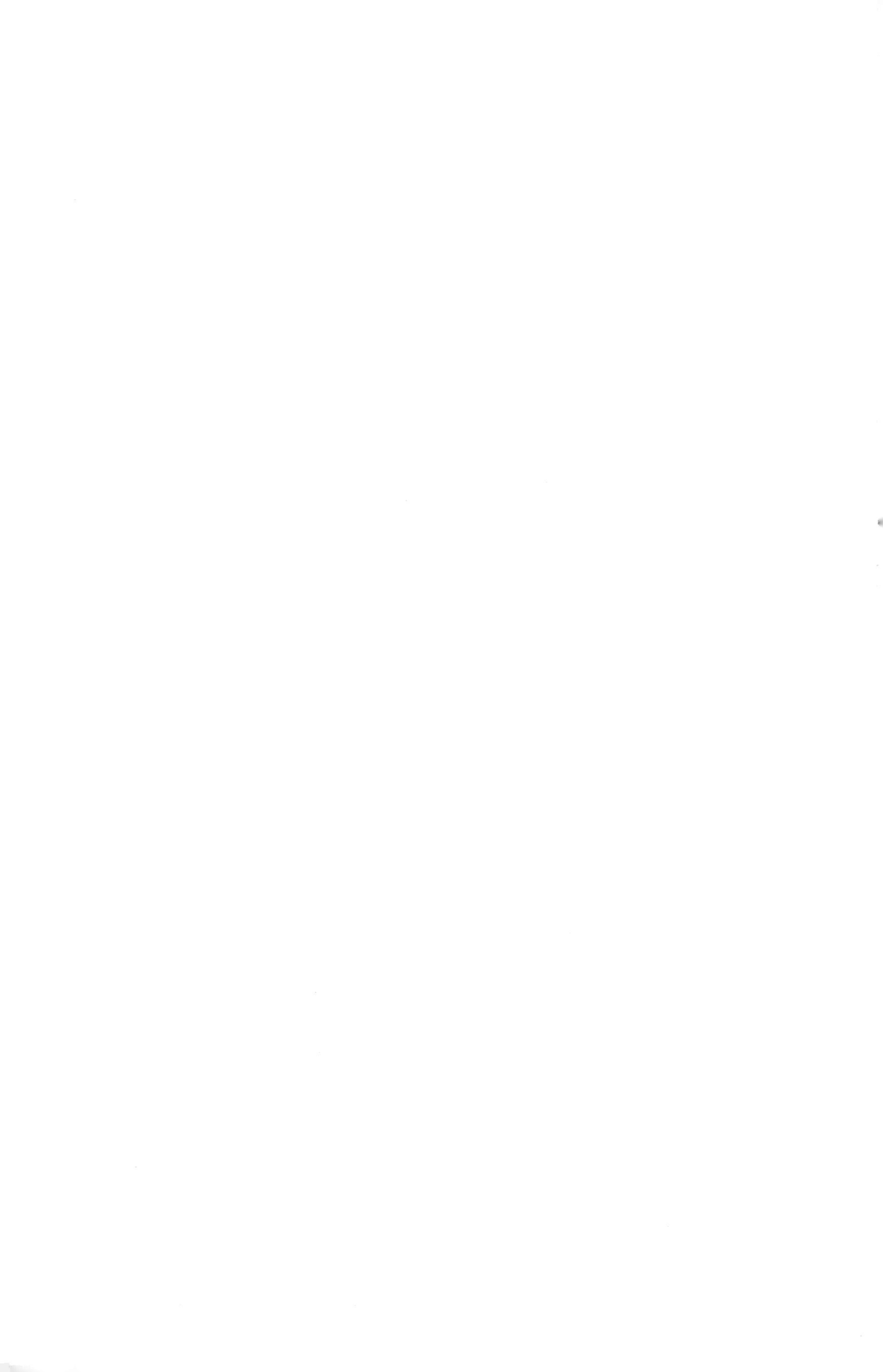

HUNTINGTON CHRONICLES

JAMES E. CASTO

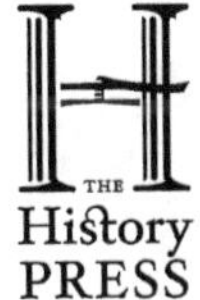

Published by The History Press
Charleston, SC
www.historypress.com

First published 2018

ISBN 9781625859662

Library of Congress Control Number: 2017963240

Notice: The information in this book is true and complete to the best of our knowledge. It is offered without guarantee on the part of the author or The History Press. The author and The History Press disclaim all liability in connection with the use of this book.

CONTENTS

ACKNOWLEDGEMENTS

This book would not have been possible without the cooperation of a number of individuals who must be thanked.

Ed Dawson, then editor and publisher of the *Herald-Dispatch*, made it possible for me to rummage in the newspaper's archives for the photographs and information required in my quest to document Huntington's history. "I'm sure Andrea can help you find what you need," he said, and online editor Andrea Copley-Smith did exactly that, smilingly responding to my many, many requests. Thank you, Ed and Andrea.

For more than twenty-five years, *Huntington Quarterly* magazine has helped chronicle our community's story. Throughout the magazine's long history, editor Jack Houvouras has enthusiastically supported my research into local history. Many of the historical profiles included in this collection originally appeared in the pages of *HQ*. Thank you, Jack.

Archives and Special Collections at the Marshall University Library is a treasure-trove of vintage photographs and other materials, and Professor Nat DeBruin and Jack Dickinson have always been quick to respond when I've turned to them for help. Thank you, Nat and Jack.

Finally, I would be sadly remiss if I failed to thank my loving wife, Norma, who's always the first to read everything I write when I say "Hon, could you look this over for me?" Norma may never have had a journalism class, but she's turned into a first-rate copyeditor. Thank you, Norma!

INTRODUCTION

My name is Jim, and I'm a history addict.

For more than thirty years, I've been researching and writing about the people, places and events that make up the history of my hometown: Huntington, West Virginia.

I'm by no means a trained historian. My bachelor's degree is in journalism, and my master's is in English. (Ask me sometime about "English Literature Before 1066.") What happened was, when I researched and wrote my first local history book, I got bitten by the bug. One book led to another, and now, nearly a dozen books later, I'm a history addict.

The story behind that first book is perhaps worth repeating. One day early in the 1980s, I was in my office at the *Herald-Dispatch* when I got a long-distance phone call from a publishing company in California. (You remember long-distance calls, don't you? It's the way we communicated back before e-mail, Facebook, LinkedIn, Skype, etc.) It seems the company was working with the Huntington Chamber of Commerce to do a coffee-table book on Huntington history. The chamber had suggested that I might be interested in writing the text and gathering the photos to include. After some negotiation, I signed a contract to do so. But I had a problem. I had just agreed to do a book on a subject I really knew precious little about. I knew the city of Huntington had been founded by rail tycoon Collis P. Huntington of the Chesapeake & Ohio Railway and that we had a very nice statue of him down at the old C&O passenger station. But that's about all I knew.

So I took myself to the local history room at the Cabell County Public Library and barricaded myself there. I also sought out people who obviously knew more about the city's history than I did. Ultimately, I was able to complete the book, *Huntington: An Illustrated History*, which was published in 1985.

I then set out on the local speaking circuit, talking to civic groups, church socials and the like about the book. And I noticed that when I opened the floor to questions, people often asked me about Collis P. Huntington. They wanted to know more about the man who founded their town. So, I redrafted my remarks to concentrate mostly on him.

Ultimately, I heard about the "History Alive!" program of the West Virginia Humanities Council. The program sends costumed reenactors out in the guise of famous personages from history. Over the years, I had done a bit of amateur theater, and so it proved a short step for me to go from talking *about* Huntington to portraying him. I'm no longer involved in "History Alive!" but from time to time can still be prevailed upon to again put on my black frock coat, my stovepipe hat and my paste-on beard and bring the old guy to life.

I delight in telling audiences about how Huntington, after playing a successful—and highly profitable—role in construction of the long-dreamed-of Transcontinental Railroad, came to the rescue of the all-but-bankrupt Chesapeake & Ohio. In 1869, the little railroad desperately needed new capital to rebuild the damage it suffered during the Civil War and push its tracks westward from Richmond, Virginia, to the Ohio River, where passengers and cargo could be readily transferred between the railroad and the Ohio's riverboats. The C&O's board of directors turned to Huntington, who made them an offer they couldn't refuse; he said he would gladly supply the new funds needed—if he was made the railroad's president. The board quickly agreed.

Huntington, his brother-in-law Delos W. Emmons and a handful of C&O officials then traveled over the mountains and across the then-new state of West Virginia to personally inspect the proposed route to the Ohio. Arriving at the river, Huntington shunned the existing little communities and instead picked out a mostly vacant tract of riverbank. There, he set about building a new town that would be the C&O's western terminus. Not surprisingly, the new town was named Huntington.

The site he selected was just downstream from the mouth of the Guyandotte River, not far upstream from where the Big Sandy River flows into the Ohio and the three states of West Virginia, Kentucky and Ohio meet. At Huntington's direction, Emmons purchased twenty-one farms, totaling five thousand acres, and hired Rufus Cook, a Boston civil engineer, to design a town plan. On February 27, 1871, the West Virginia legislature approved an act incorporating the City of Huntington. The community grew rapidly and by the early 1890s had a population of more than ten thousand.

Huntington is known for its broad, tree-lined streets; for Ritter Park, fashioned from land originally intended for use as a city incinerator; for the handsome Cabell County Courthouse; and for its many fine church buildings. Huntington is home to dozens of congregations, including seven located in a six-block stretch of downtown Fifth Avenue.

Like other towns, Huntington has had its ups and downs over the years. The city boomed during the 1920s. But the good times came to an abrupt end when the stock market crashed in October 1929. Of the eleven banks operating in Huntington during the 1920s, only two survived the Great Depression. It took the outbreak of World War II to put Huntington, like the rest of America, back to work. The city's factories shifted to war production and operated twenty-four hours a day, seven days a week.

With the war's end, the 1950s proved to be a decade of remarkable growth and achievement for Huntington—the city's zenith, some would argue. Sadly, in the decades following, Huntington saw many factories close, businesses slump and jobs disappear. Part of the decline stemmed from a sweeping decline in West Virginia's coal mine employment as automation took hold, and part was attributable to the same "rust belt" woes experienced by so many cities.

The city's economic woes have been reflected in a dramatic population decline. In 1950, Huntington had more than eighty-five thousand residents. Today, it has fewer than fifty thousand. Some people simply moved to growing suburban areas outside the city, but many left the region, seeking better opportunities elsewhere.

The Huntington of the 1950s is gone and isn't coming back. But it would be a serious mistake to argue that the city's best days are behind it. There's much that today's Huntington can be proud of and encouraged by—the dramatic growth of Marshall University, the city's rise as a major medical center and, of course, the construction of Pullman Square, the retail/restaurant/entertainment complex that's breathing welcome new life into the downtown.

In 1869, Collis P. Huntington stood on the banks of the Ohio, looked out over a tract of vacant river bottomland and envisioned a busy city, one teeming with stores and factories, schools and homes. Today, the rail tycoon's dream is very much alive and well.

PART I

THE EARLY YEARS

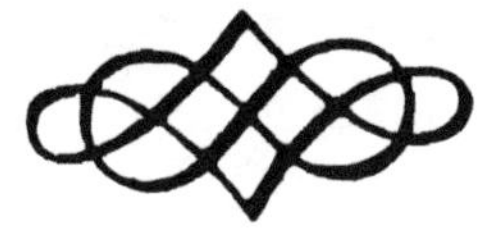

THE LIFE AND TIMES OF COLLIS P. HUNTINGTON

The life of Collis P. Huntington, founder of the city of Huntington, reads much like the rags-to-riches stories popularized in the Horatio Alger novels of his day.

Born on October 22, 1821, in rural Connecticut, the future rail tycoon was one of nine children born to farmer William Huntington and his wife, Elizabeth. The Huntington family farm was stubbornly unproductive, and in fact, the pretty little glen where the farm was located was known as Poverty Hollow.

His boyhood friends would later recall that the young Huntington loved to wrestle, besting all the other boys around and on one memorable day tussling with a teacher. Huntington himself loved to tell the story of that day:

> *The penalty in our school for bad spelling, as fixed by Mr. Peck, the teacher, was one blow of a heavy ruler on the palm of the hand for every word misspelled. I was never in those days, or am now, much of a speller....So one day I agreed with four other boys that when the spelling lesson came up, we would all miss every time. We did so....And when we were called up to the front of the class for punishment, two of us went for that teacher and whipped him.*

Huntington's schooling came to an abrupt end shortly thereafter. His father apprenticed his fourteen-year-old son to a neighboring farmer. His pay? Seven dollars a month, plus room, board and work clothes. The next year, he went to work for another neighbor, a grocer, and there he learned the rudiments of buying and selling.

He put aside every penny he earned, and when he had accumulated a bankroll of $175, he set out as a Yankee peddler. He bought a stock of simple goods, loaded some of them on his back in a couple of leather knapsacks and then walked from farm to farm, selling what he could as he stopped at each. He continued to save his money, enabling him to buy a horse and then a wagon so he could carry a larger selection of merchandise.

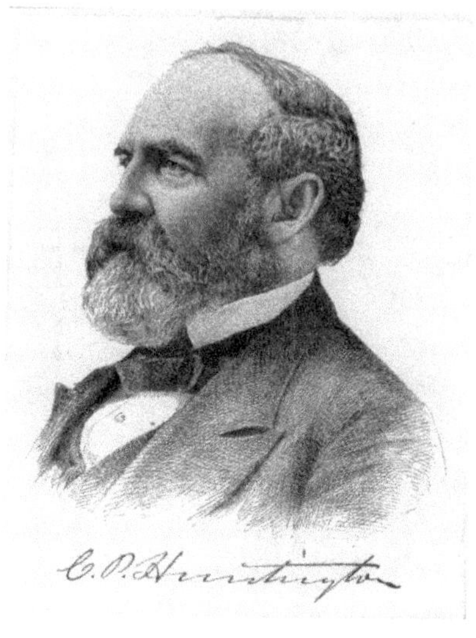

Rail tycoon Collis P. Huntington never lived in Huntington, West Virginia, but without him, the city would not exist. *Library of Congress.*

Huntington married and settled down, buying a half-interest in a general store his older brother Solon opened. And he might have been content to spend the rest of his days as a small-town merchant had not an important event taken place in California in 1848. Gold was discovered at Sutter's Mill and, like thousands of others in the East, Huntington determined to go west and seek his fortune. And Huntington did indeed make a fortune in California—not by mining gold but by mining the miners. He sold his half of the general store to his brother Solon and took his share, not in cash, but in merchandise—the very tools and supplies the miners would need in their quest for gold.

Like many others, Huntington went to California by ship, first sailing down to Panama, traveling westward across Panama on horseback and then boarding another ship on the Pacific side and continuing north to California. All the while, he had that initial stock of merchandise with him. Huntington briefly inspected the gold fields and then settled in Sacramento. The town was booming, with real estate prices soaring. Huntington found he couldn't afford to buy or even rent a building. So he set up an open-air shop on a vacant lot and found a huge demand for his goods, even at the outrageous prices he charged. As his stock dwindled, he quickly wired his brother to send more. Before long, he did rent a building and continued doing a brisk business.

In 1855, Huntington had the good fortune to meet and go into partnership with a man, Mark Hopkins, who would be his friend and associate for more than twenty years before Hopkins's untimely death. Their Sacramento store,

Huntington & Hopkins Hardware, prospered. Some have called Huntington a "natural-born salesman." Similarly, Hopkins was a born bookkeeper with an uncanny head for figures.

Soon, the two men began expanding their horizons beyond the hardware business. They both played leading roles in the launching of the Republican Party in California. And they were constantly on the lookout for opportunities to invest the considerable profits their store was generating. That being the case, it's perhaps inevitable they would become interested in the new railroads that were being built on every hand.

In 1860, Huntington and Hopkins joined with two other California businessmen, Leland Stanford and Charles Crocker, to finance construction of a few miles of California railroad. That was the beginning of what would become a mammoth railroad empire. Little wonder that railroad historians refer to the four men as the "Big Four."

The four divided up their responsibilities: Crocker supervised the actual railroad construction sites. Stanford, who became governor of California, took care of the partners' interests on the California political scene. Hopkins kept the books (some of which mysteriously disappeared when Congress later started looking into the partners' dealings). And it fell to Huntington's lot to deal with Congress and the New York banks and brokerage houses that the partners had to enlist in their efforts.

Huntington was thirty-nine years old at the time. He had never had any particular interest in railroads. But as fate would have it, they would be at the center of his life for the next forty years.

In 1862, Huntington was able to convince Congress that he and his partners should be commissioned to build the western half of the long-proposed Transcontinental Railroad. Their railroad, the Central Pacific, started laying track at Sacramento, heading east. The rival Union Pacific began laying its track at the Missouri River, heading west. It would take seven years, tens of millions of dollars and hundreds of lives lost in construction accidents along the way, but the two sets of track finally met at Promontory Point, Utah, on May 10, 1869.

The elaborate ceremonies there that day included the driving of a golden spike to link the rails. A historic photograph was taken, showing the many officials gathered to witness the spike ceremony. Collis P. Huntington isn't in the photo. He wasn't there. He was back in his New York office writing his partners an irate letter about the money needlessly spent on the gala celebration. That was typical of Huntington, always known as a slow man with a dollar.

On completion of the Central Pacific, Huntington and his partners turned their attention again to California and began to forge another rail line, the Southern Pacific, which eventually would far surpass the Central Pacific in size.

Meanwhile, the reverberations from driving the golden spike in Utah had hardly died away when a delegation representing the C&O Railway called on Huntington in his New York office.

People long had dreamed of connecting the James River and the Ohio River. At first, the thought was to do so by building a series of canals. But that didn't prove feasible. With the advent of railroads, this was a perfect spot to build one. And a bold start was made. But then the Civil War erupted. Marauding troops, Union and Confederate alike, tore up the tracks, dynamited many of the locomotives and burned the rolling stock. The result was that the C&O was all but bankrupt and desperately needed new capital to rebuild. Huntington agreed to supply the necessary money—if the C&O would install him as president. The railroad's board readily agreed. Significantly, Huntington purchased control of the C&O on his own, without his California partners.

Huntington knew that if the C&O was to ever make a profit—indeed, if it was to survive much longer—the tracks had to be pushed over the mountains and across the then-new state of West Virginia to the Ohio River as quickly as possible. In keeping with other C&O officials, Huntington set off to personally explore the new railroad's proposed right-of-way and select a location for its western terminus on the Ohio.

Many people in the village of Guyandotte, located where the Guyandotte River flows into the Ohio, were certain Huntington would pick their little town as the C&O's terminus. They were to be disappointed in that hope. Legend has it that Huntington bypassed Guyandotte due to something that befell him there.

As the story goes, Huntington and his companions arrived at Guyandotte on horseback, spied a boardinghouse and decided to stop there for a drink. They tied up their horses outside. But while the party was inside, Huntington's horse, rather than continuing to stand in the street, somehow managed to climb up on the wooden boardwalk in front of the place. At that point, the mayor of Guyandotte happened along and saw the horse standing on the boardwalk. Entering the boardinghouse, he demanded to know whose horse that was outside, blocking the way. Huntington said it was his, and the mayor fined him five dollars.

Huntington paid him on the spot—and the next day, the citizens of Guyandotte were sorely disappointed to learn their little town wasn't going to be the western terminus of the new C&O. It's a funny story, but it's likely a myth. There's no evidence it really happened.

In any event, Huntington and the rest of his party ventured a bit downriver from Guyandotte, where there was a nice tract of bottomland that appeared to be a good spot for the Ohio River's steamboats to land and connect with the future railroad. Huntington had invited his brother-in-law Delos W. Emmons to accompany him on the trip, and he instructed Emmons to buy as much of the river bottom as possible. Huntington had a vision—a vision of an entirely new town to be constructed at the site he had selected.

He hired a well-known Boston civil engineer, Rufus Cook by name, to draw up a town plan, instructing him to use a precise grid-like pattern with broad avenues and intersecting streets, each consecutively numbered so that any address might be easy to find. (Interestingly, he directed that two of the town's avenues be a good deal wider than the others. And that's why Third Avenue and Fifth Avenue are, as Huntington ordered, "broad enough to turn a team of oxen in them.")

In February 1871, the new town of Huntington was incorporated. Much of the land in the new town was reserved for the railroad. Construction crews built a handsome passenger depot, a locomotive shop and housing for the railroad's workers. Huntington and Emmons formed the Central Land Company and began selling building lots for businesses and houses. Demand for them proved brisk.

A locomotive, Greenbrier by name, was floated down the Ohio on a barge. And just as was done for the Transcontinental Railroad, crews started laying two sets of track. One set started in Richmond, Virginia, heading west. The other began in Huntington, heading east. The two sets of track met at Hawk's Nest, West Virginia. No golden spike there. Not on Collis Huntington's railroad.

In 1882, Huntington extended the C&O's tracks eastward to Newport News, Virginia. This meant that West Virginia coal destined for foreign sale could be shipped to Newport News and loaded at the C&O's piers into oceangoing freighters. When those freighters proved hard to find, Huntington founded the Newport News Shipyard to build them.

Also in the 1880s, Huntington pushed the C&O west from Huntington to Cincinnati and absorbed smaller railroads at a rate that outpaced the C&O's

abilities to pay for them. In 1887, a bankruptcy sale was averted when banker J.P. Morgan stepped in and took control. That ended Huntington's role with the C&O.

But Huntington remained firmly in charge at the Central Pacific and the Southern Pacific, as well as at the Newport News Shipyard. As his death neared, he owned vast tracts of land in California, West Virginia, Mexico and Guatemala, along with railroad investments in Mexico, South Africa and Australia.

On his death in 1900, the *New York Times* estimated his wealth at $70 million. Translated into today's dollars, that would be far more than $1 billion and perhaps close to $2 billion. Not bad for a man who started out selling what he could carry on his back.

THE DAY THE FIRST TRAIN ARRIVED IN HUNTINGTON

January 29, 1872, was a red-letter day in Huntington—the day the first train arrived in Huntington from Richmond, Virginia, then the eastern terminus of the Chesapeake & Ohio Railway. Workers had built a handsome passenger depot in the new town, and it was ready and waiting for that first train.

Eight days before the train's arrival, a committee chaired by J.G. Breslin, the first ticket agent at the new depot, had met to draft plans to give it a royal welcome. The committee included Peter Cline Buffington, the city's first mayor; Delos W. Emmons, town founder Collis P. Huntington's brother-in-law who managed the rail tycoon's business affairs in the new town; and John Hooe Russel, a banker known primarily as Huntington's most eligible bachelor.

The committee planned a gala celebration, including a one-hundred-gun salute. But the telegraph lines along the C&O route between Huntington and Richmond were disrupted, so the gentlemen in Huntington lost contact with the train and couldn't be sure when it would arrive.

When word came that the train was about to arrive, the committee's best-laid plans went for naught. But as word of the arrival spread, a crowd of several hundred people gathered at the depot and sent up a loud cheer as it pulled in.

Aboard the train were various VIPs, including General William Carter Wickham, the C&O's vice president and the man responsible for interesting Collis Huntington in investing in the all-but-bankrupt railroad. Also aboard

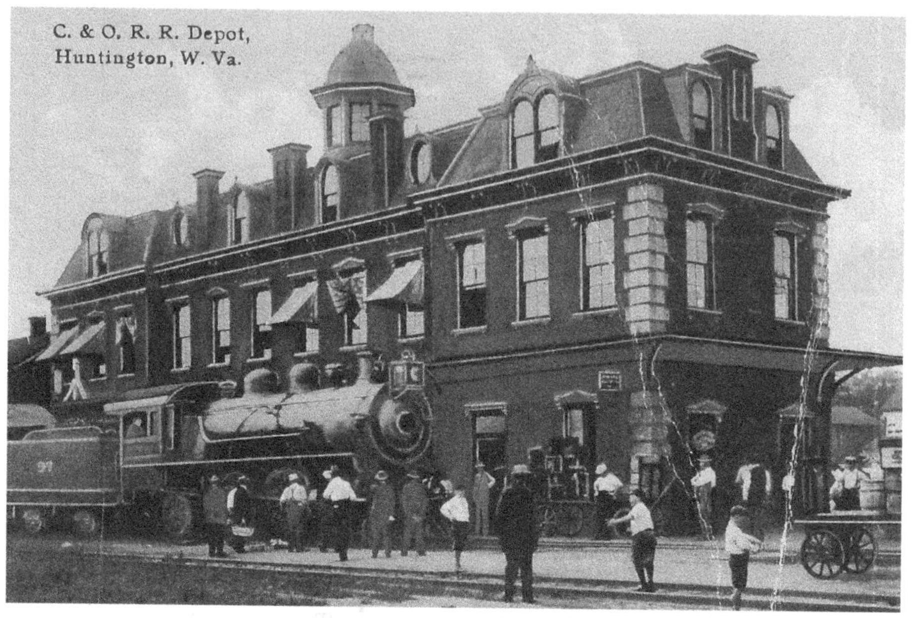

The newly constructed Chesapeake & Ohio passenger station in Huntington was ready and waiting on January 29, 1872, when the first C&O train arrived from Richmond, Virginia. *Author's collection.*

was a newspaper reporter from a Richmond newspaper, the *Daily Dispatch*, who later penned an account of the trip. The surviving copy of his account is incomplete but begins with a stop at Barboursville, located along the track just a few miles outside Huntington:

> *At Barboursville, we stopped in response to a telegram from Mr.* [John] *Laidley, who bountifully supplied the party with egg-nog and splendid apples and cigars....*
>
> *Our engineer* [Thomas A. Hall] *had orders to answer the cheers that greeted us along the route. Entering fully into the spirit of the thing, he gave vent to his whistle and made the hills echo the glad news that the first train from Richmond had arrived.*
>
> *Huntington had prepared for a grand reception. A meeting of the citizens had appointed committees to arrange for firing one hundred guns, having the city illuminated, and celebrating the glad event with other fitting celebrations. But the telegraph lines were down and as they did not learn until after night that the last rail had been laid near Hawk's Nest, they concluded to postpone their celebration.*

When we dashed into the city at 11 o'clock that night, but few of the citizens knew of our coming, but a number met us at the depot and gave us a most hearty greeting.

After a comfortable night's rest in our sleeping car, which we preferred to the hotel, we accepted hospitalities of the Ware House and got there an excellent breakfast before doing Huntington. We had but little time as our train was to leave at 11:30, but under the guidance of two old Virginia friends, we saw a great deal in that time.

Eighteen months ago, there was not a house in the present limits of the city save two frame houses. But it being decided that the Chesapeake & Ohio would tap the Ohio there, an enterprising land company bought 5,000 acres and had it laid off into a city five miles long and two wide, broad streets and a magnificent riverfront, along which a fleet of steamers can anchor.

At the head of reliable navigation on the Ohio, the most convenient shipping point of the finest coal region in the world, the terminus of the great trunk line that must carry so large a part of the trade between the great West and the deepwater and prospective center of a network of railroads. Huntington was called by one of our party, "the city of magnificent distances, vast capabilities and great expectations."

The shops of the company where they propose to make well nigh everything in the way of cars and their magnificent roundhouse, which are located here, would of themselves, go far in the making of a city, but when we remember how near it is to cheap coal and iron, there seems no doubt her "great expectations" are well founded, that her "vast capabilities" will be properly utilized and her "magnificent distances" filled with business houses and private residences.

Already the city has a population of 3,000, which is rapidly increasing. The citizens are from every section of the United States and, indeed, from every quarter of the globe, but seem entirely harmonious in its opinion that Huntington is to be a great city and united in the purpose of making it such.

The railroad runs up to the river and by means of a stationary engine transfers freight to the steamers from the cars in the shortest time imaginable. Already freight often accumulates so rapidly that they have to work all night to move it and there will be a very great increase in it now that the road is through and the regular lines of steamers have been established.

But we hurried from this goodly city and the company of pleasant friends and at 11:30 are speeding our way homeward over one of the smoothest, finest roads of the continent and through magnificent country. Along the

> *whole route we are greeted with cheers, waving handkerchiefs, etc., and at one point an old woman waved a large sheet on a pole.*

The train's trip back to Richmond was a slow one. The dignitaries aboard spent much time inspecting the industry in the Kanawha Valley and touring the region's coal mines. They marveled at the scenery through the New River Gorge and had numerous meetings with potential railroad users.

The day the train finally arrived back in Richmond was declared a holiday. All business was suspended while a big parade made its way through the city. And the train received a one-hundred-gun salute like the one planned but aborted at Huntington.

On its trip to Huntington, that first train had carried a demijohn that had been filled with water from the James River. The demijohn was emptied into the Ohio and filled again. On its return to Richmond, the train carried that container of Ohio River water, which, on the train's arrival, was emptied into the James—thus symbolically "marrying" the two rivers.

THE STORY BEHIND THE HUNTINGTON STATUE

The statue of town founder Collis P. Huntington that stands in front of the city's former Chesapeake & Ohio Railway passenger station on Seventh Avenue has been a familiar local landmark since it was erected in 1924. Yet odds are that few who glimpse the statue can name the gifted artist who sculpted it.

The Huntington statue was created by Gutzon Borglum, one of the most acclaimed sculptors of his day.

Born in 1867, Borglum first studied art in San Francisco and then in Paris, where he met and began a longtime friendship with the great sculptor Auguste Rodin. Back in this country, Borglum did many well-received works, including a memorial to Pickett's Charge at the Gettysburg battlefield, statues of angels and saints at the Cathedral of St. John the Divine in New York City and a massive head of Lincoln at the U.S. Capitol. But his name will forever be associated with the Mount Rushmore Monument.

Borglum was retained by the United Daughters of the Confederacy to do a monument to Robert E. Lee at Stone Mountain in Georgia, but disputes between Borglum and the businessmen directing the project prompted his dismissal. In 1923, Doane Robinson, the state historian of South Dakota, read of the Stone Mountain venture and wrote to Borglum about the possibility of doing a mountain carving in the Black Hills. Borglum embraced the idea and would spend the rest of his life creating the giant heads of Washington, Jefferson, Theodore Roosevelt and Lincoln that make up Mount Rushmore. Borglum died in 1941, and it was left to his son Lincoln to finish the work.

How did an artist who would go on to create an American icon such as Mount Rushmore first do a statue of railroad tycoon Huntington? That's an intriguing story—one that's even tinged with a hint of scandal.

Elizabeth, the rail tycoon's first wife, died in 1883, and the following year, he married Arabella "Belle" Yarrington, who had a son, Archer by name. Huntington adopted the fourteen-year-old boy, saying, "I couldn't love him more if he were my own son." Here's where a whiff of scandal comes in. The gossips of the day insisted that Arabella had been Huntington's mistress for years and that Archer was, in fact, his son.

Whatever the true relationship between Collis and Archer, Collis was clearly a surrogate father to his favorite nephew—Henry, the son of his brother Solon. When Solon appealed to his brother to find a suitable job for the young man, Collis dispatched Henry to St. Albans, West Virginia, where he put him in charge of a sawmill that produced railroad ties for the C&O. Henry's performance there greatly impressed his uncle, who saw to it that he swiftly rose in the ranks at the C&O. Henry ultimately was to prove every bit as canny as his uncle Collis, amassing a fortune of his own. He was one of the first to see the profit potential in investing in Los Angeles real estate, and when he started building and buying streetcar lines, he ended up owning virtually every line in California.

Collis P. died in 1900, and his will split the bulk of his fortune—estimated at $70 million—between his widow, Arabella, and his favorite nephew, Henry. At this point, some newspapers described her as "the richest woman in America." It was Arabella and Henry who commissioned the Borglum statue.

Arabella Huntington died in 1924. Six weeks after her death, the statute of Collis was unveiled in his namesake city. Henry was scheduled to attend the ceremony on October 23, 1924. But only days before the event, he telegraphed his regrets. Instead, he dispatched Homer L. Ferguson, president of the Newport News Shipbuilding & Dry Dock Co., to represent him. Collis was the shipyard's founder.

A crowd estimated by the *Advertiser* newspaper at more than seven thousand people jammed the area around the C&O station to witness the ceremony.

The Huntington Boy Scout Band performed a program of patriotic tunes, and Dr. M.L. Wood, pastor of the Fifth Avenue Baptist Church, delivered the invocation. Mrs. Mary Parsons Shrewsbury pulled the ribbon that unveiled the statue. Newspaper accounts identified her as the city's closest relative of the Huntingtons but didn't specify her relationship.

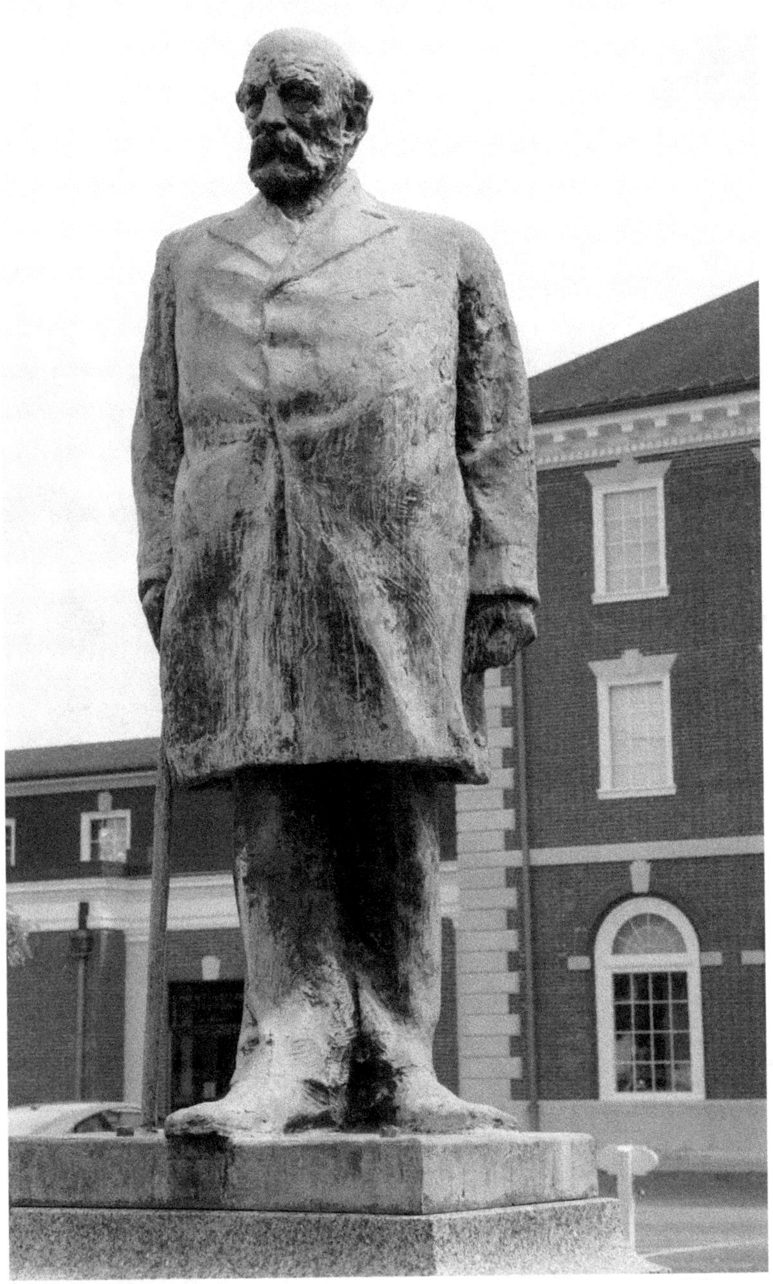

Dedicated in 1924, the statue of Collis P. Huntington that stands at the city's former C&O station was done by famed sculptor Gutzon Borglum. *Herald-Dispatch.*

In a lengthy speech filled with praise for both Huntington the man and Huntington the city, Ferguson presented the statue jointly to the railroad and the city. "Mr. and Mrs. Henry E. Huntington are the donors," he said.

Borglum did not attend the ceremony. Nor did Archer Huntington and his wife, Anna. A talented sculptor in her own right, Anna Hyatt Huntington had studied with Borglum and had recommended that he be commissioned to do the statue.

Borglum's Collis P. Huntington statue quickly became a familiar part of the city scene and stood in front of the C&O station for more than fifty years. In 1977, when the city's former Baltimore & Ohio Railroad passenger station and freight depot was turned into the restaurant/retail complex known as Heritage Station, the Huntington statue was moved there. One wonders what the often blunt-spoken rail baron would have said about being memorialized at a rival railroad station.

In 1999, at the request of CSX Transportation, the statue was returned to the former C&O station and its place of honor there.

BANK OF HUNTINGTON ROBBED!

While many experts on western history are dubious, local legend blames Jesse James and his gang for the daring holdup of the Bank of Huntington on September 6, 1875.

Missouri-born Jesse and his brother Frank were Confederate guerrillas during the Civil War, leaving a bloody trail wherever they rode. After the war, they turned to crime, robbing banks, stagecoaches and trains, often in partnership with fellow outlaws Cole Younger and his brothers John, Jim and Bob, as well as other former Confederate raiders. With each brazen robbery, the gang's notoriety grew. Eventually, their names would become automatically linked to virtually every robbery that took place.

Maybe it was the James-Younger Gang and maybe not, but the Huntington robbery clearly fit their pattern. The gang's style was to hold up a bank in the middle of the day, with well-armed men and good, fast horses. Thus, four riders made their way into Huntington on the afternoon in question. When they tied their horses to the hitching rack across the street from the bank, two men stayed with the horses and the two others strode into the bank.

Cashier Robert T. Oney was the only person in the little two-story bank when the robbers entered. Ordinarily, John Hooe Russel, the bank's president, would have been there, but he was at lunch.

Once inside the bank, the two gunmen jumped over the counter. Oney lunged for a pistol that was lying on a desk, but he wasn't fast enough. One of the gunmen grabbed it. Pointing his own pistol at Oney's head, one of the gunmen demanded that he open the safe. He said it was already open. The two said they wanted the inside compartment opened. Oney said he didn't have the key. Searching the desk, the robbers found the key.

Outside, the other two gunmen started firing pistols up and down the street, sending the few people around scurrying for cover.

Inside, the two robbers told Oney to take the key and open the safe. He refused. "If you don't, we will kill you," one said. "If you kill me, you won't get the money," Oney replied. But the standoff was a brief one. Staring down the barrel of a gun, Oney decided to open the safe. The robbers scooped up the money, later said to be $20,000. One gunman asked Oney if any of the money belonged to him. He said he had a $1 checking account. The robber threw him a dollar bill before he and his companion exited the bank.

Mounting up, the four bandits first trotted down the dirt street at a leisurely pace and then sped up and rode out of town at a full gallop, waving their hats in the air.

Returning from lunch, Russel saw the two men exiting the bank and immediately realized what had happened. As they rode away, he rushed into the bank, grabbed a shotgun and quickly headed for his horse.

Within ten minutes of the robbery, Russel, Cabell County sheriff D.J. Smith and twenty armed men were in hot pursuit of the culprits. At the same time, George F. Miller, the bank's executive vice president, was alerted by telegraph and quickly set out from nearby Barboursville with a second posse.

The gunmen rode hard out Eighth Street Road toward Wayne and then crossed the Big Sandy River into Kentucky. The first posse gave up and returned to Huntington empty-handed the next day. In later years, Sheriff Smith often told how, when his posse got close to the robbers, he had ordered an immediate charge, only to have some of his men insist they had to dismount and tighten their saddle girths. Miller's posse kept up the chase for three more days but also failed to catch up with the four.

The robbers had made a clean getaway from West Virginia, but one was later fatally wounded in a shootout with lawmen in Kentucky and another was captured in Tennessee. In both instances, cashier Oney went to the scene and identified each man as one of the Huntington bandits. The dying man refused to give his name, and the captured bandit gave an obvious alias. He admitted his role in the Huntington robbery but refused to identify his criminal companions. He was convicted of the robbery and sentenced to fourteen years in the West Virginia Penitentiary at Moundsville. Paroled in 1883, he quietly disappeared.

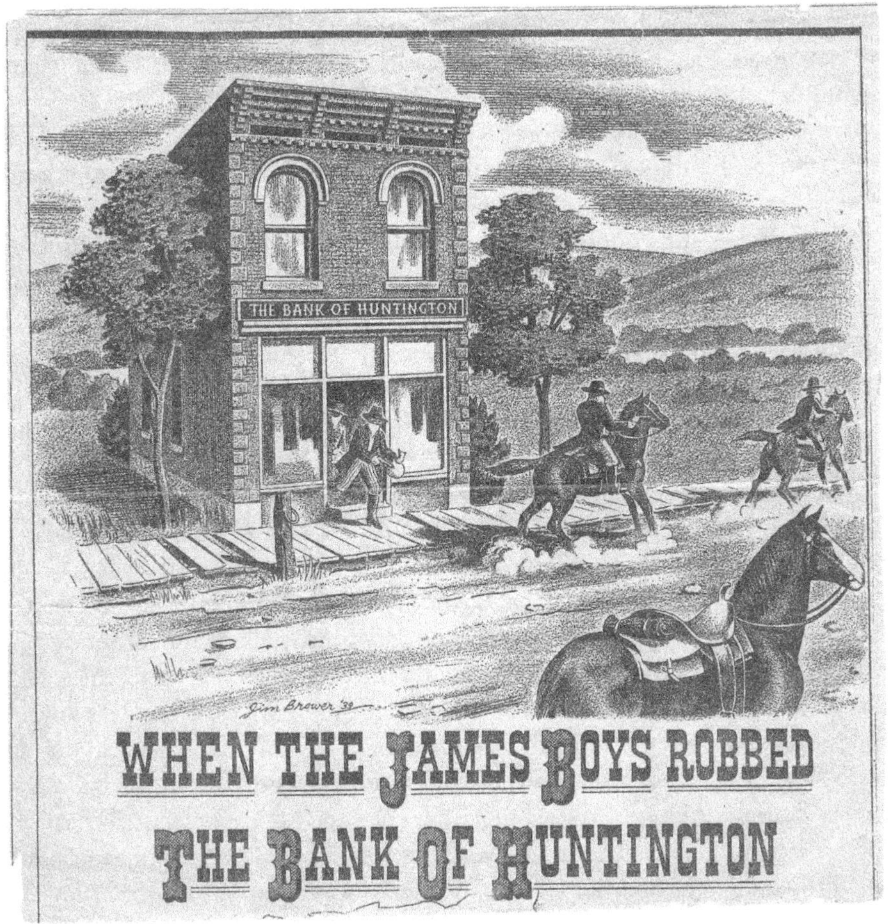

Local legend says it was famed bandit Jesse James and his gang who robbed the Bank of Huntington on September 6, 1875. *Herald-Dispatch*.

Detective Delos T. "Yankee" Bligh of Louisville long waged a campaign to bring the famed outlaws to justice. Learning of the Huntington bank robbery, he immediately wrote Russel, providing their photographs and descriptions. Russel replied: "Your description answers to all the parties who were here in the bank and were on the outside during the robbery."

From that time forward, the Huntington robbery would forever be linked with the "James Gang" and the "Younger brothers."

In 1975, exactly one hundred years after it was robbed, the Bank of Huntington building was jacked up from its foundation, put on wheels and moved from its original location on Third Avenue to the nearby Heritage Station historical center. Still standing, the old building has over the years been home to a variety of businesses.

Here's an intriguing footnote to the Huntington bank robbery: in August 1903, famed bandits Frank James and Cole Younger visited Huntington as part of a traveling Wild West show.

Frank James surrendered to authorities in 1882, shortly after his brother Jesse was killed by Bob Ford. Frank was put on trial but never convicted of any of the several charges against him. Cole Younger was paroled in 1901 after serving twenty-five years of a life sentence for robbery and murder. In 1903, the two decided to cash in on their notoriety. Teaming up with a Chicago showman, they formed "The Great Cole Younger & Frank James Historical Wild West Show" and set out on tour.

Wild West shows were tremendously popular at the time. "Buffalo Bill" Cody took his spectacular show not only to cities across the United States but in Europe as well. The show James and Younger put together was a pale imitation of Cody's but nevertheless did well for a couple of seasons.

After the show's thirty-three-car railroad train pulled into Huntington, there was a street parade with cowboys and Indians and other performers. But the main attractions were James and Younger themselves. Crowds followed them wherever they went. And, of course, people wanted to know about the 1875 bank robbery in Huntington, long rumored to be the handiwork of the James-Younger Gang.

"I am as innocent of complicity of the robbery of the Huntington bank as a little babe," James piously vowed when questioned by a reporter for the *Huntington Advertiser*. "Not only have I been unjustly accused of robbing the Huntington bank but many others as well."

James said he had been warned not to visit Huntington lest he be called to account on the old robbery charge. But no attempt was made to arrest him or Younger. The well-attended afternoon and evening performances of their show went on as scheduled, and the former outlaws and other performers then boarded the train for the show's next stop.

NEW YEAR'S DAY 1913 BROUGHT BRIDGE TRAGEDY

It's been more than one hundred years, but the tragedy that took place in Huntington on January 1, 1913, is one that's still talked about when railroaders and rail fans get together to swap stories.

A Chesapeake & Ohio Railway Company crew was working on the C&O bridge over the Guyandotte River that morning when a locomotive started across it, heading from Guyandotte to Huntington. The locomotive had just about reached the bridge's midpoint when the middle span collapsed underneath it, plunging the locomotive, engineer E.B. (Shorty) Webber of Russell, Kentucky, and thirteen bridge workers into the icy water below. Seven of the bridge workers survived, but Webber and six of the workers were killed.

Until then, the journey from Hinton, West Virginia, to Russell, Kentucky, had been routine for Train No. 99, a manifest freight hauled by Mikado engine No. 820. There was no hint of the disaster that lay ahead.

When the train reached the Guyandotte Bridge, a flagman signaled it to stop. According to an account of the accident published in the May 1994 issue of the *Chesapeake and Ohio Historical Magazine*, the train's head brakeman, A. Williams, asked bridge foreman Rufus Meadows why they had been stopped. Meadows replied that they were being held up because a work train on the bridge was unloading material for his repair crew.

Brakeman Williams and fireman J.R. Cook had walked out onto the bridge when they saw the flagman signal Webber to proceed across. Webber eased the train onto the bridge, intending to pick up Williams and Cook on the other side.

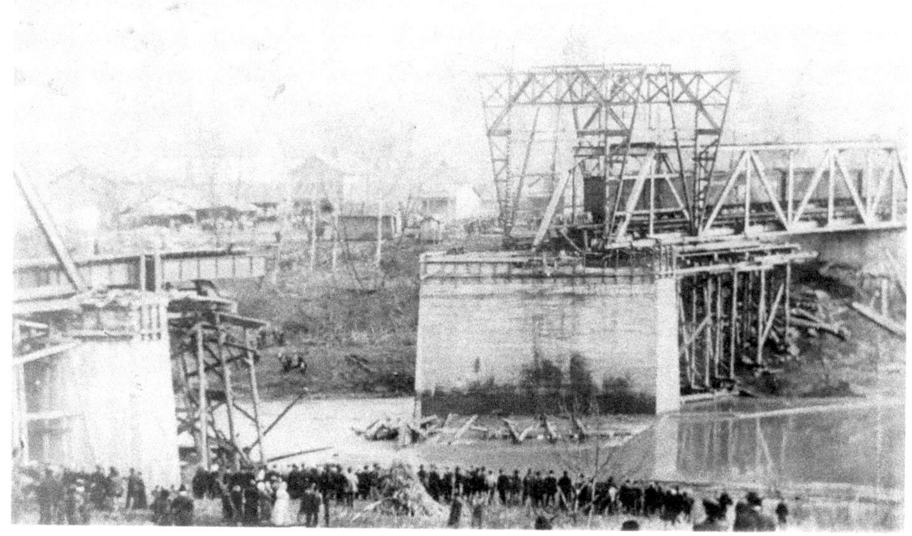

On January 1, 1913, a C&O locomotive started across the Guyandotte River but never made it to the other side. *C&O Historical Society.*

Webber—married and a father of nine—no doubt felt he was safe, as work on the bridge had been underway for several days, with trains crossing the span as usual. But that wasn't the case this time. Eyewitnesses testified that the locomotive first listed to one side, and then the entire structure under it gave way. When the engine fell, it took its tender and one boxcar with it.

The January 2, 1913 issue of the *Herald-Dispatch* offered this account of what followed:

> *More than a score of workmen on the bridge were hurled into the water, and many had thrilling escapes from what seemed certain death. The uninjured aided in the rescue of their companions who were hurt, swimming with them through the icy water to the shore.*
>
> *Within a few minutes after the crash occurred, hundreds of persons attracted by the noise, hurried to the scene and assisted in the work of rescue.*

A number of physicians rushed to the scene, including virtually the entire staff of the Huntington C&O Hospital.

The six bridge workers killed were identified as Henry "Jaybird" White of Guyandotte; Emmett Wood and Charles Maddy, both of Talcott, West Virginia; Charles Coyner of Teasy, West Virginia; J.G. Wheeler of Milton, West Virginia; and J.W. Crawford of St. Albans, West Virginia.

The bridge crew had been at work expanding the C&O's single track to a double track and in the process had constructed a series of temporary piers. The thinking was that high water had weakened the piers, causing the collapse.

A special C&O train brought three professional deep-sea divers to the scene from Norfolk, Virginia, to search for the victims. But only the bodies of engineer Webber and bridge worker Crawford were immediately recovered. Later, the body of bridge worker Maddy washed ashore fifty miles downriver at Portsmouth, Ohio.

Crowds of people—sometimes numbering into the thousands—lined both sides of the river as the search continued for bodies. The *Huntington Advertiser* reported: "A man with a moving picture machine was on the scene...and took several films of the crowds and the incidents following the disaster."

By spring, all hope of recovering the remaining bodies had been given up. Then, on May 24, two boys boating on the Guyandotte discovered the body of bridge worker Wood in the water only a short distance from the accident scene. The other bodies were never found.

Work started immediately on repairing the bridge. Meanwhile, the C&O contracted with the Baltimore & Ohio Railroad to temporarily use its nearby bridge across the Guyandotte.

Recovering the locomotive that had plunged into the river proved to be a Herculean task. One of the heaviest engines then in use by the C&O, it had disappeared into the water and buried itself in a thick layer of muddy sand at the river's bottom. Initial attempts to pull engine No. 820 from the river failed, and a decision was made to wait until the river receded. Finally, on June 29, nearly six months after the disaster, the engine—described as "a sorry sight, nothing left but the boiler on wheels and mud all over"—was pulled from the water and taken to the Huntington shops. There, it was rebuilt and then placed back in service.

THE 1913 FLOOD WAS WORST EVER–UNTIL 1937

The 1913 Ohio River flood was the worst to ever hit Huntington—until the devastating 1937 flood.

Flood stage at Huntington is 50.0 feet. On March 31, 1913, the Ohio, which had been steadily rising for days, crested in Huntington at 66.4 feet. That was the city's highest crest ever recorded until that time. The 1913 record stood until the 1937 flood topped it by nearly 3.0 feet, cresting at 69.2 feet.

There had been Ohio River floods before, of course. When the first settlers made their way into the Ohio Valley in the early and mid-1700s, they found the river was subject to dramatic changes. When the weather was dry for weeks at a time, it could be so shallow that one early settler described it as "a mile across and a foot deep." At some points, you could walk across it and hardly get your feet wet. Yet in periods of heavy rainfall or when a sudden thaw quickly melted the accumulated winter snow from the nearby hillsides, the Ohio could become a raging torrent.

Major Ohio River floods were recorded in 1862, 1883 and 1884, when the river washed away an estimated two thousand homes along its length. Although it hardly seems a laughing matter, people familiar with the Ohio and its history joke about the firehouse in Marietta, Ohio, that was swept away, fire engine and all, by a raging flood and, six days and many miles later, "turned up as part of the Louisville Fire Department."

The Ohio flooded again in 1901 and 1907. Then, in March 1913, it rained steadily for five straight days over much of the Ohio Valley, and the Ohio

River and its tributaries began rising rapidly. The flood hit Parkersburg and Point Pleasant hard, and soon it was Huntington's turn. High water quickly flooded Huntington's downtown business section along Second, Third and Fourth Avenues. An estimated five hundred citizens were marooned in Guyandotte.

"Never since the flood of 1884 has the city of Huntington been in worse condition," warned the March 30 edition of the *Herald-Dispatch*. Churches, schools and other public buildings soon were crowded with an estimated two thousand men, women and children who had been driven from their homes.

No lives were lost in the 1913 Huntington flood, but suffering was acute. Fuel, light and gas supplies were cut off entirely. The city's water mains had to be closed to keep out the floodwaters. J.M. McCoach & Company came to the community's rescue when it temporarily linked the city's water system to the artesian well at its refrigerated warehouse on Seventh Avenue at Thirteenth Street.

Governor Henry D. Hatfield ordered two companies of the West Virginia National Guard to patrol the flood-stricken city to prevent looting. At the same time, Mayor Floyd S. Chapman deputized one hundred well-known citizens as auxiliary police. They were given special blue ribbon badges to wear and were told they would be serving without pay.

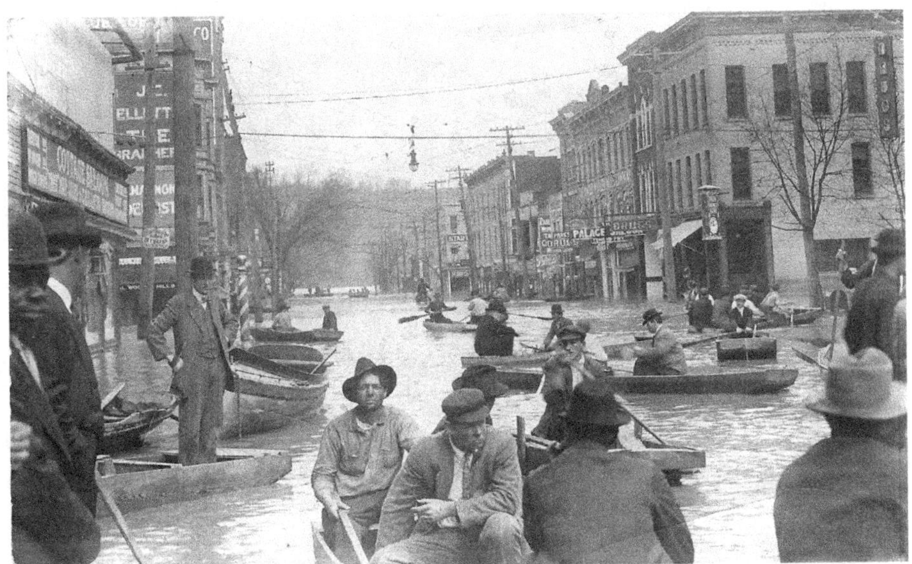

The Ohio River left its banks and inundated much of Huntington in March 1913. Here's a view of the flooded downtown intersection at Fourth Avenue and Ninth Street crowded with rowboats. *Author's collection.*

Mayor Chapman ordered that all the city's saloons be closed. However, the *Herald-Dispatch* reported that the city's bootleggers continued to do a brisk business. Chapman also directed the city's banks to close for three days (March 29–31). As flood refugees crowded Oley School, three babies were born there.

The Reverend U.V.W. Darlington cancelled Sunday morning services at Johnson Memorial Methodist Church, saying, "I think this is the time to practice Christianity rather than preach it." The women of the church used a basement kitchen to prepare food for free public distribution.

"Charleston responded nobly with carloads of provisions, boats, fire engines, and a force of practiced firemen, boatmen and general helpers," the *Herald-Dispatch* reported.

Meanwhile, the city's newspapers were having their own troubles.

The floodwaters forced the *Herald-Dispatch* out of its building. The newspaper set up a temporary newsroom at the Chesapeake & Potomac Telephone Company, where the staff worked by candlelight and oil lamps. Type had to be laboriously set by hand, and then the newspapers were printed on a hand-operated press at the Blagg Printing Company.

The rival *Advertiser* managed to stay in its building but had to convert a natural gas engine to one using gasoline in order to power its printing press. Both newspapers had to deliver their papers by boat.

WORLD WAR I TROOP TRAINS GOT WARM WELCOME IN HUNTINGTON

When the United States declared war against Germany on April 6, 1917, President Woodrow Wilson urged his fellow citizens to help the newly formed American Red Cross assist the thousands of young men joining the Allied forces on the battlefields of Europe. The Red Cross responded in a number of ways, but surely the most widely known and longest remembered was by providing coffee, snacks and personal items for members of the military crisscrossing the country on troop trains.

During the war and for months after the fighting ended, Red Cross volunteers—almost all women—operated seven hundred canteens at railroad passenger stations across the nation, with several in West Virginia. One of the busiest was in Huntington at the Chesapeake & Ohio Railway station at Seventh Avenue and Ninth Street.

The Huntington canteen opened on September 9, 1918, and closed exactly a year later. Even though the Armistice ended the war just two months after the canteen opened, the troop trains kept coming, carrying thousands of men on their way home or, in some cases, to hospitals. So the canteen workers remained on the job to help them.

A small army of 650 volunteers worked at the Huntington canteen under the direction of Lula Wellman Mossman, the canteen's commandant, who was the wife of prominent Huntington businessman Dan A. Mossman. In the early months of the war, Lula and a group of her friends met in the basement playroom of her Sixth Avenue home to make bandages for the wounded overseas. When the Huntington chapter

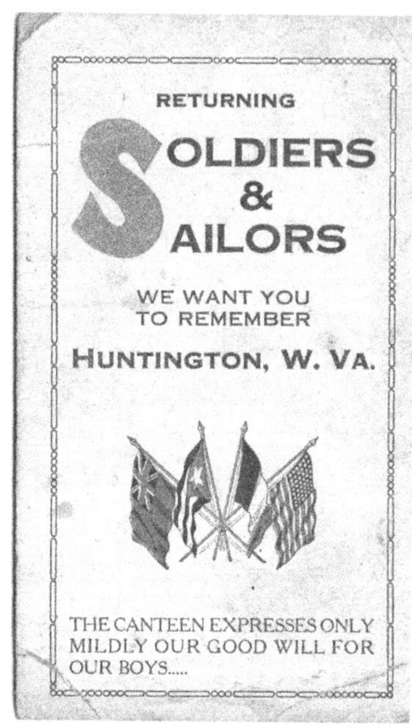

When World War I ended, troops whose trains stopped at the Red Cross canteen were given pamphlets urging them to come back to Huntington and settle down. *Author's collection.*

of the Red Cross set about opening its canteen, she was a logical choice to take charge.

The Huntington Lumber & Supply Company donated a small wood building that was moved to the C&O station. Volunteers had to be at least twenty-three years old. They were divided into groups and strictly scheduled. Each woman had to be certified by the Red Cross and outfitted in a long white uniform, with a white apron and head covering with the Red Cross emblem. A volunteer motor corps was organized for those who had no way of getting to the station and then back home.

The troop trains pulled into the station for a brief stop at all hours of the day and night, and a dozen or more women met every train, even those that arrived at 3:00 a.m. or so. The women prepared the food items, cleaned the building (known as "the hut") and went aboard the trains to invite the men to come to the canteen and to serve the wounded men who couldn't leave the train.

The food was plain but hearty—sandwiches, homemade cake or pie, candy, fruit, milk and, of course, coffee. The women also passed out free cigarettes, pipe tobacco, magazines and postcards. At the canteen's height, the women served an average of about 5,000 men a week. The record for one day was 2,333 men.

Food for the canteen was donated by townspeople and local businesses. Others donated money so the volunteers could buy what was needed. Almost daily, Huntington's newspapers published lists of donors and what they had supplied. On a day when three troop trains had gone through, the published list included the names of thirty-nine people who made contributions, large and small—a jar of jelly, one or more pies, quantities of milk, two dozen eggs and three dozen doughnuts, plus gifts of money.

At one point, the canteen was notified to expect seven hundred soldiers for supper. The meal was served at the National Guard Armory. Most of the food was donated. One hotel supplied the meat and another hotel supplied the vegetables. Plates and silverware were loaned by stores, and the soldiers were served by seventy canteen volunteers.

The Red Cross enthusiastically praised the cooperation rendered the canteen by the C&O: "They arrange to let the boys stay here as long as possible every time." The commanding officer of one train refused permission for his men to be served at the canteen, saying they needed exercise more than food. He then proceeded to march them up and down the street.

The canteen had its share of poignant moments, as reported in the daily newspapers. For instance, one soldier, when he realized he was in Huntington, remarked that he had a brother working at C.M. Love Hardware whom he hadn't seen for several years. A bystander hurried off to the hardware store, and shortly before the troop train pulled out, he returned with the soldier's brother in tow. The two men hugged and had a great reunion, while the crowd cheered.

When the war ended, the canteen remained a busy place, as the volunteers helped soldiers on their way back to their homes. Sensing a marketing opportunity, the Huntington Chamber of Commerce printed and distributed thousands of small leaflets praising the city and urging the returning soldiers, once they were discharged, to come back and settle down.

"Hurry home and see your folks and your girl," the leaflets advised. "Then pack your grip and come back and grow up with us. There's a hearty welcome here always for the right sort. We are building the biggest and best town on the Ohio River between Pittsburgh and Cincinnati and are only sorry that you cannot drop off and look it over."

The chamber leaflet also urged that soldiers share it: "Hand this card to some manufacturer who is looking for the best located factory town in the country. Tell him to write us and challenge us to prove the assertion, and we will do it conclusively."

When the canteen finally closed, a newspaper noted it had been a great success "largely through the untiring efforts of Mrs. Dan A. Mossman, canteen commandant." Until her death in 1964, Mrs. Mossman regularly received grateful thanks from many former soldiers who recalled the warm welcome they received when their train stopped for a few minutes in Huntington.

USS *HUNTINGTON* CARRIED DOUGHBOYS HOME

Not one but two U.S. Navy warships have been named for Huntington, West Virginia. The first served with distinction in World War I. Construction of the second began at the height of World War II but wasn't completed until the war's end. Both ships long since have gone to the scrapyard.

This is the all-but-forgotten story of the first USS *Huntington*. In one of those odd twists of history, it was actually named the *West Virginia* when it was launched at the Newport News Shipbuilding Company on April 18, 1902. Katherine White, daughter of West Virginia governor Albert White, broke the traditional bottle of champagne against its bow.

Completed and commissioned in 1905, the armored cruiser *West Virginia* was one of the largest warships of its day. Built at a cost of more than $6.8 million, it was five hundred feet long, with a beam (width) of sixty-nine feet and a displacement of 13,400 tons. It bristled with guns and boasted nine inches of armor plate. At top speed, it could make an impressive twenty-two knots.

Petty Officer H.C. Winn kept a journal of his time aboard the ship and in 1919 published it under the title *Fighting the Hun on the USS Huntington.* Winn had a good eye for detail, and his journal does much to supplement the dry-as-dust prose of the official navy record. For example, President Theodore Roosevelt traveled aboard the *Huntington* from New Orleans to Hampton Roads, Virginia, in October 1905. In his journal, Winn recorded that during his trip, Roosevelt visited the ship's engine room, where he tried his hand at

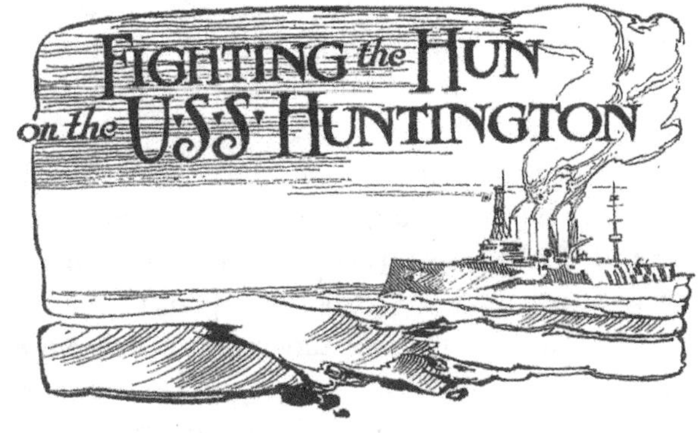

Petty Officer H.C. Winn kept a journal of his time aboard the USS *Huntington* and published it with this title drawing. *Author's collection.*

shoveling coal. The shovel he used, Winn noted, was later hung in the engine room as a souvenir of the occasion.

In 1916, the Mexican rebel Pancho Villa crossed the U.S. border and raided the sleepy little town of Columbus, New Mexico, killing more than a dozen Americans. In response, President Woodrow Wilson sent General John J. Pershing and six thousand troops into Mexico and ordered a naval show of strength along Mexico's western coastline. The fleet that steamed into Mexican waters included the *West Virginia*, and it was there it was renamed the *Huntington*.

The official navy history indicates a decision had been made to build a new class of battleships and give them state names, so the *West Virginia* had to be renamed. But the history is frustratingly silent on how *Huntington* was chosen as the ship's new name. Launched in 1920, the new *West Virginia* was badly damaged in the Japanese attack at Pearl Harbor on December 7, 1941, but was rebuilt and fought on until the end of the war. But that's getting ahead of our story on the *Huntington*.

In February 1917, the *Huntington* was anchored at Mare Island Navy Yard in California, where it was fitted to accommodate four seaplanes to be launched from a steam catapult mounted on the quarterdeck. On their return, they would land in the water and be hoisted back aboard by crane. The *Huntington* was one of the navy's first ships to be so equipped.

About 350 men composed the ship's peacetime crew. In April 1917, when word came that war had been declared with Germany, the navy ordered all ship commanders to immediately increase their number of men to a wartime total. For the *Huntington*, that meant the recruitment of an additional 300 sailors. Civilians were enlisted directly on the ship and received all their training shipboard.

Sailing from the Pacific to the Atlantic via the Panama Canal, the *Huntington* spent two months at Pensacola, Florida, testing its new catapult launching system. Then it was assigned to convoy duty, escorting troopships carrying doughboys to France.

In addition to its seaplanes, the *Huntington* was one of the first ships in the U.S. fleet to be equipped for the launching of observation balloons. On September 17, 1917, one of those missions nearly ended in tragedy. A manned balloon had been sent aloft. When a sudden squall forced the balloon down into the water, its basket capsized and rolled over several times. Lieutenant (Junior Grade) Henry W. Hoyt was trapped underwater in the balloon's rigging. Ship's Fitter First Class Patrick McGunigal quickly leaped from the cruiser's deck into the raging water, rescuing the balloonist. In recognition of his heroic action, McGunigal was awarded the Medal of Honor, the first awarded during World War I.

On the *Huntington*'s return home from its first convoy mission, a decision was made to remove the catapult and the four aircraft, which had been plagued with problems since being put aboard. Shortly thereafter, the *Huntington* carried a high-level American delegation across the Atlantic to confer with the Allies on the conduct of the war. The fifteen-member delegation was headed by Colonel Edward M. House, an advisor to Woodrow Wilson who had such a close relationship with the president that he had his own living quarters at the White House. (In his journal, Winn noted that House brought along his wife and her maid.)

In all, the *Huntington* made nine eastbound nine trips across the Atlantic, escorting sixty-two troopships carrying an estimated total of more than 175,000 troops. During those crossings, the ship frequently sighted German submarines on the surface and opened fire on them. Official reports credited the gun crews of the *Huntington* with sinking four German subs.

Winn described one encounter with a sub:

> *About noon, a lookout, in the maintop, spotted a U-boat on the surface. Our port aft six-inch gun, and all three-inch guns that could bear, opened fire on the enemy, but were unable to hit the target. Suddenly the aft eight-inch turret cut loose. The explosion was tremendous as a direct hit was scored, and the submarine disintegrated. The crew celebrated the victory with a rousing cheer.*

At the war's end, the American public was demanding that their family members in uniform be returned home as quickly as possible. So the

Huntington was pressed into service as an improvised troopship. The navy stripped it of everything that could be removed so that returning soldiers could be tucked into every conceivable nook and cranny.

On its first trip in this new role, the *Huntington* carried 1,700 returning servicemen from France to New York City, landing on January 14, 1919. Nearly two dozen other warships were pressed into service as makeshift transports, but the *Huntington* boarded 200 more troops than any of the other vessels. The ship made five more voyages to France and back, bringing home a total of nearly 12,000 troops.

The *Huntington* was decommissioned in a ceremony at Portsmouth Navy Yard at Kittery, Maine, on September 1, 1920. Ten years later, in accordance with the London Treaty that limited naval armaments, it was stricken from the navy's official roster of ships and sold for scrap. Over the decades since, its story has been largely forgotten. Yet its record of service remains admirable and noteworthy.

DEADLY 1918 FLU EPIDEMIC HIT HUNTINGTON HARD

The year was 1918.

In Europe, World War I raged on. Though no one knew it at the time, the bloody conflict was nearly over. The fighting would end in November. Meanwhile, Americans here at home found themselves fighting a war of their own—a war against the worst epidemic this country has ever seen.

Worldwide, the death toll in the great influenza epidemic of 1918 is put at 20 million. In this country, the killer flu struck as much as 30 percent of the population and killed more than 500,000 people.

The 1918 flu was unlike any other. People could be seemingly healthy in the morning and dead by nightfall. Others died more slowly, suffocating from the buildup of fluid in their lungs. The deadly flu didn't discriminate. Its victims were rich and poor, townspeople and farm families alike. More than 850 New Yorkers died of the flu in a single day. In Philadelphia, the city's death rate for one single week was seven hundred times higher than normal. Soon there was a nationwide shortage of caskets.

The flu found its way to West Virginia, where it sickened thousands and killed hundreds. It's estimated that Huntington saw as many as three thousand cases and nearly two hundred deaths before the epidemic ran its course. Charleston recorded equally grim statistics.

People called it the "Spanish influenza" because it was thought to have originated in Spain. But medical experts now believe that the ailment actually originated in a less menacing virus that was spawned at army camps in this country and then carried by the American troops to the trenches of Europe,

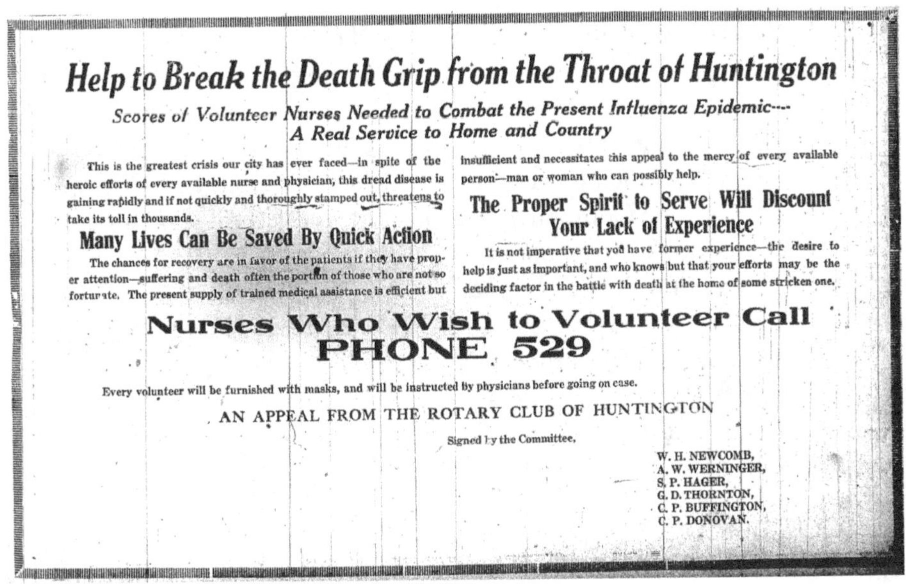
Help to Break the Death Grip from the Throat of Huntington

Scores of Volunteer Nurses Needed to Combat the Present Influenza Epidemic---
A Real Service to Home and Country

This is the greatest crisis our city has ever faced—in spite of the heroic efforts of every available nurse and physician, this dread disease is gaining rapidly and if not quickly and thoroughly stamped out, threatens to take its toll in thousands.

Many Lives Can Be Saved By Quick Action

The chances for recovery are in favor of the patients if they have proper attention—suffering and death often the portion of those who are not so fortunate. The present supply of trained medical assistance is efficient but insufficient and necessitates this appeal to the mercy of every available person—man or woman who can possibly help.

The Proper Spirit to Serve Will Discount Your Lack of Experience

It is not imperative that you have former experience—the desire to help is just as important, and who knows but that your efforts may be the deciding factor in the battle with death at the home of some stricken one.

Nurses Who Wish to Volunteer Call
PHONE 529

Every volunteer will be furnished with masks, and will be instructed by physicians before going on case.

AN APPEAL FROM THE ROTARY CLUB OF HUNTINGTON

Signed by the Committee,

W. H. NEWCOMB,
A. W. WERNINGER,
S. P. HAGER,
G. D. THORNTON,
C. P. BUFFINGTON,
C. P. DONOVAN.

At the height of the deadly 1918 influenza epidemic, the Huntington Rotary Club used the newspaper to issue a public appeal for volunteer nurses. *Herald-Dispatch.*

where it mutated into a killer. The first news reports of deaths caused by the flu came from Spain, hence the malady's name.

Returning American troops brought the mutated virus back home. First hundreds, then thousands of soldiers at army camps across the nation were felled by the often deadly disease. A news dispatch from Camp Meade in Maryland reported that in just twenty-four hours, the camp had recorded seven hundred cases and seventy-seven deaths—including nineteen soldiers from West Virginia.

On October 2, Huntington's newspapers reported the deaths of three city soldiers from the disease and noted that authorities suspected it was being spread from town to town along the railroads. "Red Cross Will Aid in Drive to Down Influenza," proclaimed a Huntington headline on October 4. The same day's issue noted that most local cases were "of the mild type."

But within days, that optimism would change dramatically. On October 8, local health officials ordered the closing of "the public schools, Marshall College, all theaters, revival meetings, billiard parlors, dance halls, and other crowded places." And the next day's issue reported the first local deaths.

"Influenza as Yet Unchecked," warned a headline on October 12, as the number of cases and the death toll began to mount. At this point, hundreds of new cases were being reported daily.

As the disease spread, the city's hospital and clinics were filled to capacity and the Salvation Army's Citadel was pressed into service to house patients. Red Cross workers made and distributed protective gauze masks to be worn over the mouths and noses of doctors and nurses. Boy Scouts were enlisted to deliver medicine from pharmacies to patients. The Chesapeake & Potomac Telephone Company, with many of its operators sidelined by the flu, appealed to the public to make emergency calls only.

Home remedies for the flu abounded. Alcohol, onion plasters, raw onions and hot lemonade were recommended. None of these treatments worked.

On October 17, the Huntington Rotary Club issued a public appeal for volunteer nurses to care for those flu sufferers who had no families to help them. "Quick attention can save lives," the news story advised. By the next day, "druggists of the city" were quoted as saying they believed the worst of the epidemic was over.

But the deadly disease had at least one more life to claim in Huntington—Mayor Leon S. Wiles, whose death was reported by the *Herald-Dispatch* on October 19. Wiles, the general manager of the Huntington Tobacco Warehouse Company, had been mayor for only a few months, having been elected the previous May. According to the newspaper account of his death, the mayor's wife and two children had been ill with the flu for some time, and with no other help available, he had been nursing them himself when he was taken ill. Like many other 1918 victims, Wiles succumbed to pneumonia brought on by the flu.

"The Great Pandemic," a website posted by the U.S. Department of Health and Human Services (1918.pandemicflu.gov), offers an anecdotal state-by-state look at the 1918 epidemic. It notes that "West Virginia University was closed…and a fraternity house on campus was turned into an emergency hospital. In Morgantown, theaters and churches were closed and public meetings banned."

The Health and Human Services site also reports the curious case of James Horvatt, a Martinsburg-area man who was arrested on charges of forging a forty-dollar check. He was put in a cell with another prisoner who had the flu. The other prisoner died, and Horvatt was sick when he was taken to court. Three lawyers who were in the courtroom that day got sick and died. The judge, the clerk and an assistant prosecuting attorney also became sick and came close to death. The record doesn't indicate if Horvatt was convicted—or even survived.

Newspaper accounts indicate that Reynolds Memorial Hospital in Glen Dale just south of Wheeling was overwhelmed by hundreds of flu patients, pushing the doctors and nurses there to the point of exhaustion and prompting a call for volunteer nurses. Seven Reynolds nurses were hospitalized with the highly infectious disease, and three of them died.

News accounts also reported the disease cut a deadly swath through the Appalachian coal fields. Some mines were forced to close for as long as six weeks because so many miners were sick and unable to work. The few able-bodied men who didn't fall victim to the disease were kept busy—not digging coal, but digging graves.

PART II

FAMOUS FACES

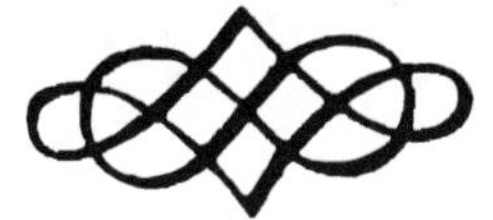

WILLIAM H. CABELL

A bit more than two hundred years ago, when the Virginia General Assembly officially established Cabell County on January 2, 1809, the lawmakers named the new county for William H. Cabell, who had served as governor of Virginia from 1805 to 1808. Surely there's more to know about a man held in such high regard by his former fellow legislators that they named a county for him.

Indeed, there *is* more to know—much more.

In 1723, Dr. William Cabell, an English physician, sailed to this country as an immigrant and settled in the Tidewater region along the James River. There, he founded a family that would play a major role in the affairs of Virginia and the nation.

Dr. Cabell's grandson would be governor of Virginia, and numerous other members of the family would be active in politics and the military. A young member of the Cabell clan is still remembered in annual ceremonies at Virginia Military Institute as one of ten VMI cadets killed at the Battle of New Market in 1864. And, although seldom read these days, James Branch Cabell (1879–1958) was a highly regarded novelist in the early twentieth century.

But that's getting ahead of our story—one that's detailed in a collection of family documents in the library of the University of Virginia in Charlottesville. There, one finds that family patriarch William Cabell (1699–1774) and his wife, Elizabeth, had five children: Mary, William, Joseph, John and Nicholas. The firstborn of Colonel and Mrs. Nicholas

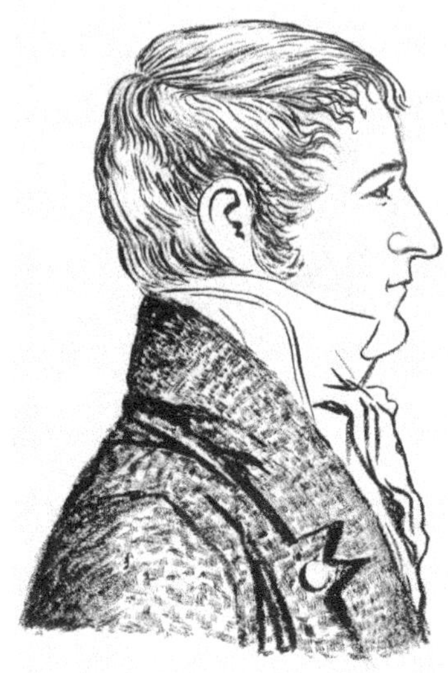

Cabell County was named in honor of Virginia governor William H. Cabell. It seems doubtful Cabell ever set foot in the county that carries his name. *Herald-Dispatch.*

Cabell was William H. Cabell, who was born on December 16, 1772. He wasn't born with that middle initial but added it himself on reaching adulthood, attempting to limit the confusion resulting from three "William Cabell"s in the family.

The future governor was extremely well educated, spending four years at Hampden Sydney College and three years at the College of William and Mary, followed by a year of legal training in Richmond, before embarking on the practice of law.

In 1795, he married his first cousin Elizabeth Cabell and moved into Union Hill, the Amherst County home of his uncle William. The local residents took a liking to the young man and elected him to the General Assembly, then regularly reelected him. Cabell's first wife died in 1801, and in 1805, he married Agnes S.B. Gamble.

From 1776 until 1852, the governors of Virginia weren't chosen by popular vote but rather by the members of the General Assembly. In 1805, they chose Cabell.

While serving as governor, Cabell worked closely with President Thomas Jefferson. When Aaron Burr attempted to organize a rebellion in the trans-Appalachian West, Cabell helped Jefferson quell the threat. He called up units of the Virginia militia to counter the insurrection, and once Burr was arrested, Cabell oversaw Burr's transfer to Richmond. There, Burr stood trial and, to the dismay of many, was acquitted.

While Burr was on trial in 1807, a British warship, the HMS *Leopard*, fired on a U.S. warship, the USS *Chesapeake*, when its captain refused to allow the British to board his ship in search of alleged deserters. Three Americans were killed and eighteen wounded. The event took place just off the Virginia coast, and Cabell, calling the attack "an outrage unprecedented in the history of nations," dispatched troops to the Chesapeake Bay area to counter a feared British invasion. War was avoided, but only for the moment, as the growing tensions between Britain and its former colony would later erupt into the War of 1812.

When Cabell completed his term as governor, he immediately took on new responsibilities as a judge. He served on the Virginia General Court until 1811 and then on the Court of Appeals until his retirement in 1851.

Like many Virginians of his day, Cabell was fascinated by the western part of the state and the economic opportunity it represented. It's no doubt that deep interest that prompted him to attend a public auction at the Eagle Tavern in Richmond, where a promising tract of river bottom along the Ohio River was offered for sale. Cabell bid $13,000 and found himself the new owner of the 4,400-acre tract located just up the Ohio from present-day Huntington.

It was Cabell's friend Judge John Coalter who, on later buying the tract from Cabell, convinced state lawmakers to create a new county and name it for Cabell. And it was Coalter who organized the new county government, doing so in April 1809 at a farmhouse owned by William Merritt located at or near the present community of Barboursville. Whether Cabell ever had an opportunity to personally inspect the new county that carried his name is unknown but seems unlikely.

Cabell died on January 12, 1853, in Richmond and is buried in that city's historic Shockoe Burying Ground. Ironically, another of the same cemetery's illustrious dead is a man whose name is also very much a part of this region's history—Chief Justice John Marshall, honored by those who in 1837 opened the humble log school building that would grow into today's Marshall University.

DELOS W. EMMONS

People in Huntington sometimes are surprised to learn that town founder Collis P. Huntington never lived in his namesake city. The famed rail tycoon's complex business dealings required that he spend months at a time in California; New York; Washington, D.C.; and other far-flung places. This meant he needed somebody he could leave in charge in the new town he had founded as the western terminus of the Chesapeake & Ohio Railway. Huntington found that man in his brother-in-law Delos W. Emmons, who had married his sister Mary. Knowing that he could spend little time in the new town, Huntington placed Emmons in charge.

Emmons, his wife and their five children briefly settled in Guyandotte while the new town took shape just downriver. In 1871, in his role as general manager of the Central Land Company, he oversaw the first sale of building lots in the new community. Later that same year, he was elected to the town's first city council.

As a council member in 1872, he was a member of the committee in charge of building the community's first two schools. That same year saw him elected as a director of the newly organized Bank of Huntington.

He bought the old Thomas Buffington house on the Ohio River, just below the mouth of the Guyandotte, remodeling it and naming it Pleasant View. There, he and his wife entertained friends and business associates. And it was there, too, that C.P. Huntington made his headquarters during his infrequent visits.

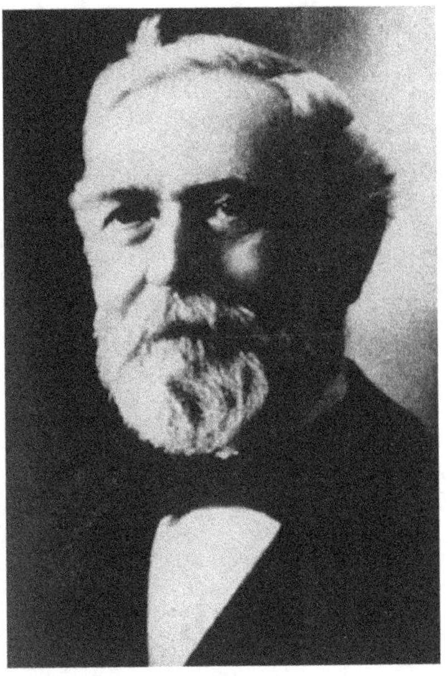

Knowing he could spend little time in his new town, Huntington needed somebody he could leave in charge in his absence. He found that man in his brother-in-law Delos W. Emmons. *Marshall University Special Collections.*

Painted a bright yellow, Pleasant View was surrounded by fifteen acres of land, on which stood elaborate horse and cattle barns. It's said that many mornings when Emmons climbed into his buggy and set off for his office, he carried with him a dozen eggs, a pound of country butter or a can of buttermilk, which he would give away to the first lucky soul he met along his way.

Three of the Emmons children played important roles in the growth and development of their adopted hometown. Arthur S. Emmons became Huntington's first city clerk and, much later, in 1912, built the Emmons Apartments at Third Avenue and Twelfth Street. J. Alden "Ollie" Emmons ran a furniture factory and in 1890 was elected an officer of the Huntington Board of Trade, a predecessor of today's Huntington Regional Chamber of Commerce. And in 1891, Carlton D. Emmons, in partnership with J.L. Hawkins, established the Emmons-Hawkins Hardware Company, which would grow to become the largest wholesale hardware company in West Virginia.

If Delos Emmons exhibited any reluctance to accept his brother-in-law's invitation to be his personal representative in the new town of Huntington, history doesn't record it. Of course, Huntington had a reputation for being highhanded, stubborn and, one way or another, almost always getting what he wanted. Thus, his "invitation" to Emmons may have been more of a command.

In any event, Emmons put down deep roots in Huntington and was one of the community's leading citizens until his death on April 19, 1905.

JOHN HOOE RUSSEL

In the Great Depression, hundreds of banks failed, and thousands of Americans saw their life savings vanish. Determined that the nation would never again witness such a sad situation, President Franklin D. Roosevelt and Congress in 1933 created the Federal Deposit Insurance Corporation, which insures the deposits in member banks.

But in the era before insured deposits, it wasn't just financial panics that endangered customers' cash. When bandits held up a bank, it was the bank's depositors who bore the loss. So, banks of that bygone day relied on iron vaults and armed guards to not only protect the bank's deposits but also assure customers that their money was safe.

Thus it was that John Hooe Russel (1842–1903), president of the old Bank of Huntington, kept a pair of ivory-handled Colt revolvers on his desk, in easy reach if needed. As fate would have it, Russel was at lunch on September 6, 1875, when four armed men—allegedly the James Gang—robbed the bank and headed out of town. At this point, Russel, returning from lunch, saw what was happening and ran into the bank for his pistols but found the robbers gone.

A chase ensued as the bandits galloped out McCoy Road (past where the Huntington Museum of Art now stands), with Russel, Cabell County sheriff D.J. Smith and twenty or so armed citizens in pursuit. The posse trailed the bandits into Kentucky before being forced to abandon the hunt and turn their worn-out horses back home.

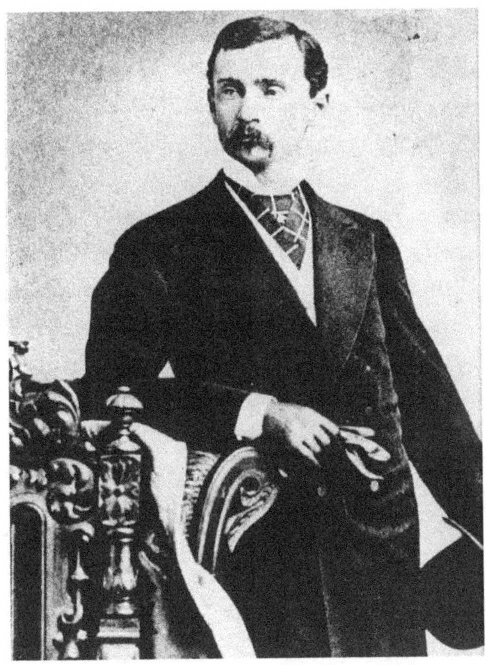

John Hooe Russel was president of the city's first bank, the Bank of Huntington. When an armed gang robbed the bank on September 6, 1875, he saddled his horse and joined the posse chasing the culprits. *Herald-Dispatch*.

The robbery provided a colorful chapter in the early history of Huntington. And, fittingly enough, in Russel it featured one of the young city's most prominent citizens.

Born in Huntsville, Alabama, on June 15, 1842, Russel was one of the first businessmen to recognize the promising opportunities available in the new city of Huntington. Arriving in the new town in 1872, Russel initially entered the grocery business, but when the Bank of Huntington (the city's first) was organized, he became its casher. He was named its president following the death of the bank's first president, Mayor Peter Cline Buffington. (Over time, the Bank of Huntington evolved into the First Huntington National Bank, one of West Virginia's leading banks.) When he took over at the Bank of Huntington, Russel was said to be the youngest bank president in the nation.

Russel was active not only in the new town's business affairs but its social circles as well. A son of the aristocratic Old South in every sense of the word, he was the chief organizer and longtime president of the Gypsy Club, known for its exclusive membership list and its elegant dances. He was one of the founders of the Trinity Episcopal Church and was a vestryman there for nearly thirty years.

His first wife was Nettie M. Phelps, of Richmond, Kentucky. She died soon after the birth of John Hooe Russel Jr., who lived only a bit more than a year. His second wife, Minerva Parke Phelps, was a cousin of his first wife. They had a son, Albert Lacy Russel, who was born in 1902 and grew up to be a prominent Cincinnati lawyer.

Local historian George S. Wallace, writing in his authoritative *Cabell County Annals and Families*, published in 1935, was high in his praise of Russel: "It was undoubtedly the presence of such men as he that was responsible, in a large degree, for the city's phenomenal growth. He had a high degree of civic pride, a keen business judgment, and through his social graces contributed much to the morale of the growing community."

ALBERT GALLATIN JENKINS

Albert Gallatin Jenkins was only thirty-three years old when he died, a victim of wounds he suffered in battle. But the young Jenkins managed to pack a great deal into his brief lifetime. He was a well-to-do planter, a Harvard-educated attorney, a member of first the U.S. Congress and then the Confederate Congress and, most notably, a daring Confederate cavalry commander. Today, his family home is a Cabell County landmark.

Jenkins was born on November 10, 1830, at Green Bottom, just a few miles up the Ohio River from the village of Guyandotte. His father, William Jenkins, was the owner of a 4,400-acre plantation, worked by more than fifty slaves, on a fertile stretch of lowland along the Ohio. It was the elder Jenkins who, in 1835, built the two-story family home that still stands on the former plantation.

Young Albert Jenkins studied at Marshall Academy and then at Jefferson College in Canonsburg, Pennsylvania, where he graduated in 1848. He went on to Harvard Law School, graduating in 1850.

Jenkins opened a law practice in Charleston but after his father's death moved back to Green Bottom, establishing a law office there. He was named a delegate to the Democratic National Convention in 1856 and served two terms in the U.S. House of Representatives.

With the outbreak of the Civil War and Virginia's secession from the Union, Jenkins resigned his congressional seat and returned to his home at Green Bottom. In an area where both Union and Confederate sympathies

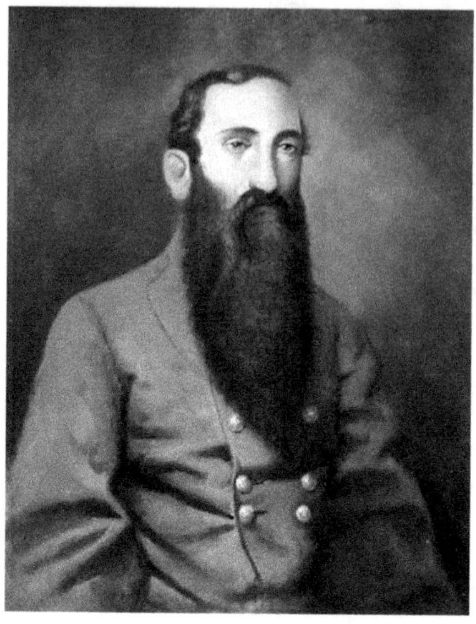

With the coming of the Civil War, lawyer Albert Gallatin Jenkins became one of the South's finest generals. Wounded at the Battle of Cloyd's Mountain, he died twelve days later. *Marshall University Special Collections.*

were strongly held, Jenkins quickly and firmly vowed his support for the Confederacy.

On April 20, 1861, Jenkins was elected captain of a volunteer company of 101 riflemen from Cabell and Mason Counties. He converted the members of the company into cavalrymen, gave them the name "Border Rangers" and arranged for their enlistment in the Confederate army.

On July 17, 1861, at the Battle of Scary Creek in Putnam County, Colonel George S. Patton (the great-grandfather of General George S. Patton of World War II fame) was in command of the Confederate troops. When Patton was seriously wounded, it was Jenkins who rallied the disorganized Confederates to victory.

In August, Jenkins formed the Eighth Virginia Cavalry, CSA, and became its colonel. In November, he joined with other cavalry units in staging a surprise raid on Guyandotte.

Early in 1862, Jenkins briefly left the field to serve in the First Confederate Congress, but he was back on duty by August, when he was promoted to brigadier general.

Civil War expert Jack L. Dickinson of Huntington, author of *Jenkins of Green Bottom*, describes Jenkins as "a fearless cavalry raider." Perhaps his most daring exploit came in August and September 1862, when he led his men on a five-hundred-mile trek through what is now West Virginia, harassing Federal troops and disrupting their supply lines. The Confederate raiders even crossed the Ohio River, becoming the first to raise the Confederate flag on Ohio soil.

Jenkins went on to command a battalion of cavalry at the Battle of Gettysburg, where he was wounded on July 2. He didn't recover sufficiently to rejoin his command until autumn. He then spent the early part of 1864 raising and organizing a large cavalry force for service in western Virginia.

Hearing that Union brigadier general George Crook had left the Kanawha Valley with a large force, Jenkins took the field against him. On May 9, 1864, he was severely wounded and captured during the Battle of Cloyd's Mountain.

In the *Huntington Herald* of June 22, 1900, E.F. Chapman wrote that he served with Jenkins and offered this account of the general's fate: "Jenkins' brigade was broken and began a hasty retreat. The General…with drawn sword, was encouraging the men to stand and cover the retreat of the other regiments of the brigade. They too fled, leaving the General alone, when he was shot from his horse and picked up by the Federal troops."

Jenkins was carried to a nearby house, where a Union surgeon amputated his arm. But Jenkins never recovered, dying twelve days later.

Writing in 1900, Chapman went on to voice a sentiment that echoed the comments of many who knew and served with Jenkins: "All in all, Cabell County never produced a more illustrious son and well may those of his comrades who still survive feel justly proud of their leader and military chieftain, who, had he lived, would have furnished material for some of the brightest pages of our state and national history."

Jenkins was initially buried at the New Dublin Public Cemetery in Virginia. After the war, he was reinterred at his home in Green Bottom. Still later, his remains were moved to the Confederate plot at Huntington's Spring Hill Cemetery.

In 1988, much of what had been the Jenkins family's land at Green Bottom was purchased by the U.S. Army Corps of Engineers to make up for the loss of wetlands taken for construction of the expanded locks at the Robert C. Byrd Locks and Dam. The corps leases 836 acres of the former plantation land to the state Division of Natural Resources, which operates it as the Green Bottom Wildlife Management Area.

The Jenkins house, located about fifteen miles north of Huntington on West Virginia 2, is subleased to the state Division of Culture and History. At one time, the house was open for public tours but was closed pending a long-delayed restoration to its mid-nineteenth-century appearance.

Jenkins Hall on the Marshall University campus is named for the general.

ELY ENSIGN

In the city of Huntington's earliest years, the young town's biggest employer was, logically enough, the Chesapeake & Ohio Railway. After all, it was the C&O that gave birth to the city when founder Collis P. Huntington picked out a tract of Ohio River bottomland to be the railroad's eastern terminus.

In those early decades, the city's second biggest employer was the Ensign Manufacturing Company.

Connecticut businessman Ely Ensign came to Huntington and established the Ensign Manufacturing Company in 1872, just a year after rail tycoon Huntington established the town that carries his name. Ensign's financial partner in the venture was a fellow Connecticut native, William Henry Barnum, a distant cousin of famed showman P.T. Barnum. Despite the company's name, it was Barnum who was president of Ensign Manufacturing, while Ensign was secretary-treasurer and manager.

Industrialist, banker, civic leader, political figure, churchman—Ely Ensign (1841–1902) was a commanding figure in early Huntington. Jack L. Dickinson has researched and written a definitive account of Ensign and the company he founded. Dickinson is the bibliographer for the Rosanna Alexander Blake Library of Confederate History at Marshall University and the author of a number of books on local history. His *Ely Ensign and the Ensign Manufacturing Company of Huntington, West Virginia* was published by Marshall's John Deaver Drinko Academy in 2013.

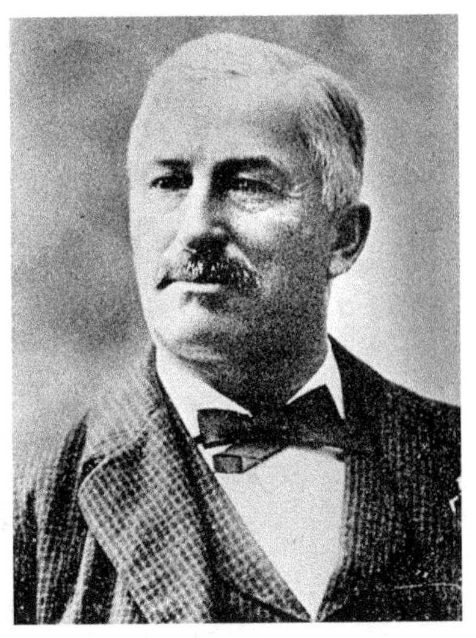

Connecticut businessman Ely Ensign came to Huntington in 1872 and established the Ensign Manufacturing Company, for many years one of the city's busiest industries. *Marshall University Special Collections.*

Fortunately for future historians, Ensign wrote many letters, telegrams and postcards to his wife, Mary, whenever they were apart. He also regularly exchanged letters with other family members and business associates. In researching his book, Dickinson was able to draw on an extensive collection of Ensign's letters and papers housed in Marshall's Special Collections department.

The Ensign collection, says Dickinson, "gives us great insight into the details of the formation and growth of not only his company, Ensign Manufacturing Co., but also of the young city of Huntington."

Dickinson also was able to draw on a microfilm collection of Collis P. Huntington's letters and papers housed in Special Collections. Both Huntington and his brother-in-law Delos W. Emmons served on Ensign Manufacturing's board of directors.

Initially, the Ensign plant produced only railroad wheels, but in 1881, it began building wooden rail cars. Within a few years, it became one of the largest car building facilities in the United States. That success may have been due at least in part to the efforts of Huntington, who, as a major investor in the C&O, the Central Pacific, the Southern Pacific and other railroads, was in an ideal position to "encourage" those lines to buy cars from the Ensign plant.

By 1895, the Huntington plant was building more than four thousand cars a year, including boxcars, stock cars, gondolas, coal mine cars and even snowplows. In 1899, Ensign was one of thirteen independent car builders consolidated into the American Car & Foundry Company (ACF). Ensign remained as general manager of the Huntington plant, continuing in that position until his death in 1902.

Ensign—generally known as "Major Ensign"—was a prominent figure in early Huntington. He was a director and vice president of the Huntington National Bank and a longtime friend of the bank's president, John Hooe Russel. In the 1880s, Ensign, Russel and a half dozen other men organized the Irving Club, a predecessor of the Guyandotte Club. He was a charter member of the Huntington Board of Trade, which evolved into today's Huntington Regional Chamber of Commerce.

A longtime member of city council, he was elected mayor in 1896. He was succeeded in that office by his son-in-law W.E. Hite, who married Ensign's daughter Anna. A decade later, his son John W. Ensign was elected mayor. One of the founders of Trinity Episcopal Church, Ely Ensign was a longtime vestryman at Trinity and was senior warden at the time of his death.

Even as other industries took root in Huntington, the ACF plant continued to play a key role in the city's economy. John Ensign followed in his father's footsteps and was manager at ACF until his death in 1932.

Over the years, the nation's railroads began replacing their wooden cars with stronger, safer steel cars. The Huntington plant was slow to make the shift from wood to steel, but once it did so, it more than made up for lost time, cranking out a steady stream of cars.

Although always best known for its railcars, ACF expanded into other fields and as a result in 1954 changed its name from American Car & Foundry to ACF Industries Inc.

In 1962, the Huntington plant began building a revolutionary new design that quickly became a standard of the railcar industry. The car, known as the Center-Flow covered hopper car, was developed by ACF to transport huge volumes of lightweight, high-bulk commodities, such as plastic pellets. By 1992, the plant had built more than 100,000 Center-Flow cars. At the peak of production, the plant was building as many as 28 cars a day.

By 2001, however, the market for the Center-Flow cars had dried up, and most of the plant's workers had been furloughed. The few who remained mostly made wheel pairs for tank cars manufactured at ACF's plant in Milton, Pennsylvania. Currently, the mostly idle plant faces an uncertain future.

JOHN HENRY CAMMACK

The name "Cammack" is one that's writ large in Huntington's history. From the city's earliest days, the Cammack family was a driving force, not just in the city's business community but in its religious and civic life as well.

Born on a farm in Dayton, Virginia, in 1843, John Henry Cammack went to school in Staunton and Lexington. In 1859, the family moved west to Clarksburg, in what would become the new state of West Virginia, where they homesteaded another farm. As a boy, Cammack attended a Sunday school class taught by Thomas J. Jackson, who would win fame as Confederate general "Stonewall" Jackson.

John Henry was seventeen when he and his brother Lucas joined the Confederate army, where he served part of his enlistment under his old Sunday school teacher. Lucas was killed in battle. John Henry, though wounded more than once, survived the war. When it was over, he walked back to Harrison County and the family farm, a trek of three hundred miles.

In 1866, John Henry married Mary Jane Fox, known to her family and friend as "Molly." The next year, they had a son, Lucius, and in 1868, they moved to Williamstown, West Virginia, where John Henry established himself as a cigar maker, a trade he had learned as a boy. In 1870, the Cammacks had a second son, Charles Walker.

At age thirty-four, he was urged by his doctor to give up cigars and find a healthier line of work. In Williamstown, he had become good friends with the Reverend W.P. Walker, a Baptist minister. When Walker moved down the Ohio River to Huntington to take charge of a newly organized church, he urged John Henry to follow him.

And so, in 1878, he bought a stock of wearing apparel and boarded an Ohio River packet steamer, the *Katie Stockdale*, heading for Huntington, where he lost no time setting up shop to sell the clothing he brought. John Henry ran his clothing store for the next twelve years until he sold it and went into the insurance business with an old friend from his army days, J.N. Potts. Later, when John Henry's son Charles Walker joined the business, it expanded into real estate development.

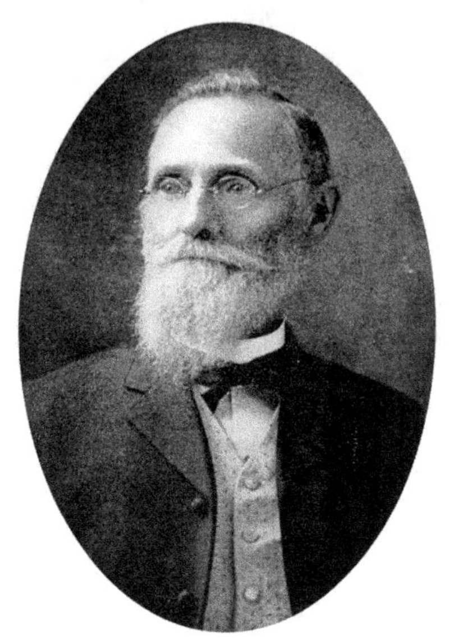

John Henry Cammack was the owner of a cigar factory when his doctor urged him to find a healthier line of work. Moving to Huntington, he opened a clothing store. *Marshall University Special Collections.*

A Baptist deacon, John Henry helped establish the Fifth Avenue Baptist Church and, later, the Twentieth Street Baptist Church.

He remained proud to have served in the Confederate cause and for many years was commander of the local unit of the United Confederate Veterans. He was still serving in the post upon his death on May 5, 1920.

The former Cammack Elementary and Cammack Middle schools on the city's historic South Side were named in his honor.

Lucius, John Henry's eldest son, was well known in Huntington as a real estate broker and a talented musician. One of the founders of what is today the Huntington Regional Chamber of Commerce, he died in 1921, not long after his father's death.

His brother, Charles Walker Cammack, worked briefly for the First Huntington National Bank before going into partnership with his father. Active with a number of local charities, he was president of the old Huntington Union Mission for twenty-seven years. On his death in 1946, the mission was renamed the Charles W. Cammack Children's Center. It remains in operation today, serving troubled youngsters—a fitting tribute to the Cammack family's concern for the community.

BRADLEY W. FOSTER

Bradley W. Foster was one of those who arrived in Huntington in 1871, the year it was born, and prospered with the young city's growth. Until his death in 1922, Foster was one of Huntington's most respected business and civic leaders. And even today, decades later, his positive influence is still felt: The Woodlands retirement community is a legacy of his remarkable generosity.

In reporting Foster's death in 1922, the *Herald-Dispatch* remarked on the helping hand he extended to many fledgling businesses: "He believed it was his duty as a citizen of Huntington to encourage business activities on the part of people newly come to Huntington by extending them financial assistance. He practiced this belief. Not a few successful men of Huntington owe their start to this confidence in his fellows and in his city."

Foster was born in 1834 in Winslow, Maine. In 1868, in Oneonta, New York, he married Mary Lenora Huntington, a niece of Collis P. Huntington, and three years later, the couple moved to Huntington, the railway town Mary Lenora's uncle had founded.

On arriving in the new town, Foster bought a plot of land on the southwest corner of Third Avenue and Eighth Street and built there a small two-story frame building that housed the B.W. Foster Hardware Company. The venture was an immediate success, and in the 1890s, the frame building came down and was replaced by a three-story brick structure. The new building would later house one of the city's best-known retailers, first named the Huntington Dry Goods Company and later renamed the Huntington

Store. Today, the Marshall Hall of Fame Café occupies the building's first floor, with office tenants on the second and third floors.

In 1906, Foster moved his hardware store to new quarters at Second Avenue and Twelfth Street, and ten years later, a merger created the Foster-Thornburg Hardware Company, a major regional wholesale supplier of hardware, furniture, plumbing and electrical supplies and appliances. The business ceased operation in 1965.

Had he done nothing else, Foster's name would stand out in the city's first half century. But he by no means confined his activities to the hardware business.

Foster was president of the Huntington Land Company, the successor to Collis P. Huntington's original Central Land Company, which owned vast holdings in the city—all the property that wasn't subdivided and sold in the city's first years. Under Foster, the company sold the land on which thousands of Huntingtonians built their homes and businesses.

He was one of the founders of the First National Bank, which became the First Huntington National Bank, for many years the city's largest. A member of city council, he was an organizer of what is today the Huntington Regional Chamber of Commerce. The chamber's first office was a room in his hardware store.

The Fosters built themselves a handsome home on the southwest corner of Fifth Avenue and Eleventh Street. Today, the site is occupied by Huntington Federal Savings Bank.

Mary Foster died in 1920. Two years later, Foster died in Florida, where he had gone to recuperate from a bout of ill health. His friend and business partner E.H. Thornburg, who was with him, told the *Herald-Dispatch* that Foster's last wish "was that he might return to Huntington to die." That wish was to go ungranted.

Foster left an estate valued at nearly $1 million, a sum equivalent to many millions in today's dollars. He and his wife had no children. Before his death, he had let it be known that he intended to leave the bulk of his estate to charity. But even his closest friends were unprepared for the extent of his generosity—an endowment of $800,000 to build a home for spinsters and widows over the age of sixty-five. Foster envisioned the Foster Memorial Home for Aged Women as a tribute to his late wife.

He created the Foster Foundation to build and operate the home and named six of his friends to the foundation's board: D.E. Abbott, E.H. Thornburg, Robert L. Archer, C.P. Snow, Rufus Switzer and Hans Watts. The board immediately set to work, picking a site on Madison Avenue between West

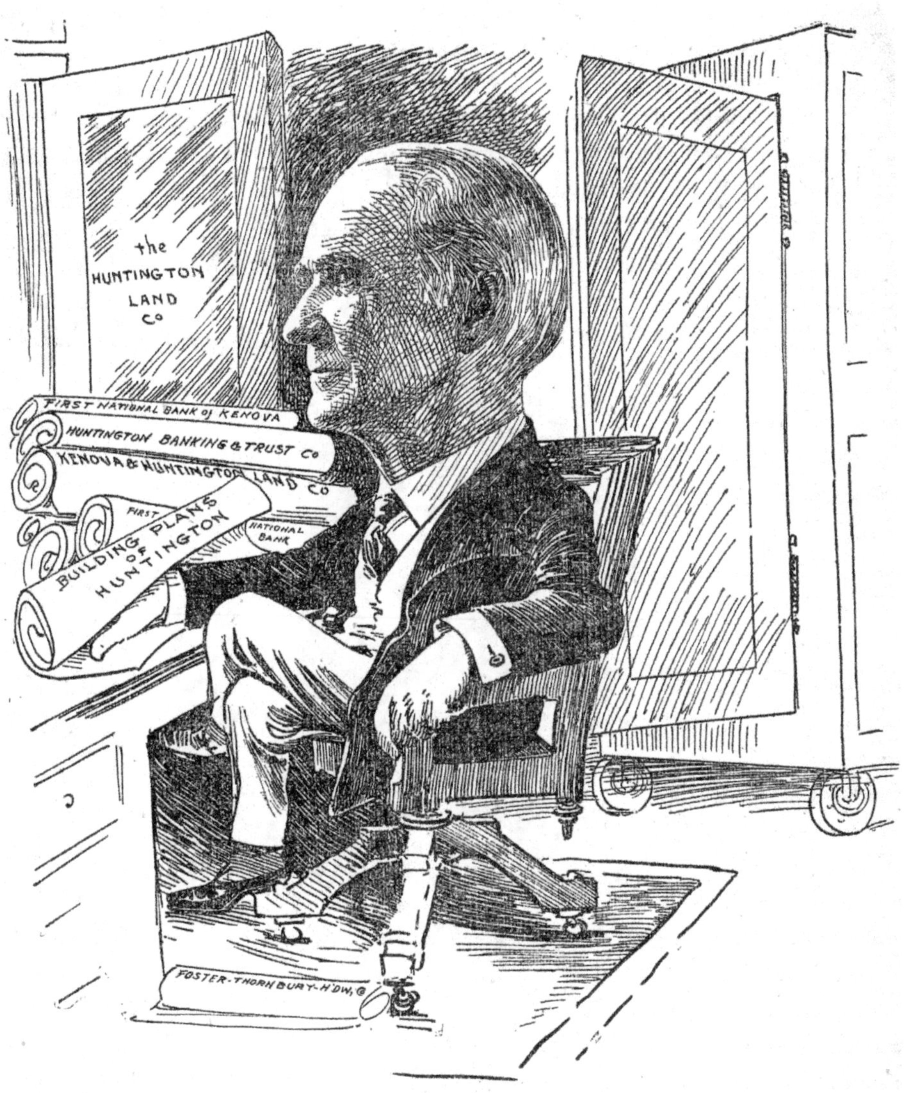

On his death in 1922, Huntington businessman Bradley W. Foster left $800,000 to build and maintain the Foster Memorial Home for Aged Women. *Author's collection.*

Seventh and West Eighth Streets and retaining prominent local architect Sidney L. Day to design the home. Day's design—a magnificent three-story Georgian Revival brick mansion that cost $250,000 to build—welcomed its first residents in 1924 and over the coming years would shelter thousands of local women.

But times change. And beginning in the 1980s, board members of the Foster Foundation began talking about the growing need for adequate housing for all seniors, not just women. The result was construction of The Woodlands, a sprawling retirement community located on 170 acres of land just off Fifth Street Road near Interstate 64.

In 1999, the Foster Memorial Home was closed and sold to a new owner who converted it to a personal care home with a new name, Regency Park. But the Foster name by no means disappeared. The Woodlands retirement community is located on Bradley Foster Drive—certainly a fitting name.

J.L. CALDWELL

Banker, Pioneer, Builder of City"—that's how a page-one headline in the *Herald-Dispatch* described Huntington's James Lewis Caldwell when he died on October 18, 1923.

J.L. Caldwell was all that and more. Much more.

He was one of the first to see the possibilities of the rich coal fields of southern West Virginia and worked tirelessly to tap that vast natural wealth. He built Huntington's first street railway and its accompanying electric lighting system. He invested in countless other business ventures in the city's early years and was long active in Republican politics.

Caldwell was born in 1846 at Elizabeth in Wirt County, then still part of Virginia. The Caldwell family hailed from Ohio, and young Caldwell was educated in the schools of Meigs County, Ohio. There, though only seventeen years old, he enlisted in the Union army as a member of Company F of the Sixtieth Ohio Infantry.

The young soldier served with distinction, taking part in the Battles of the Wilderness, Cold Harbor and Petersburg. Proud of his time in uniform, he would later serve as West Virginia commander of the Grand Army of the Republic, the once-vast organization of Union army veterans.

At war's end, Caldwell briefly represented an insurance company in Wheeling, traveling far and wide in the state. In St. Albans, he met and courted Mary O'Bannon Smith, and they soon wed. They remained husband and wife for fifty-two years. The young couple first lived in Wheeling and then moved to Guyandotte, as did Mary's parents.

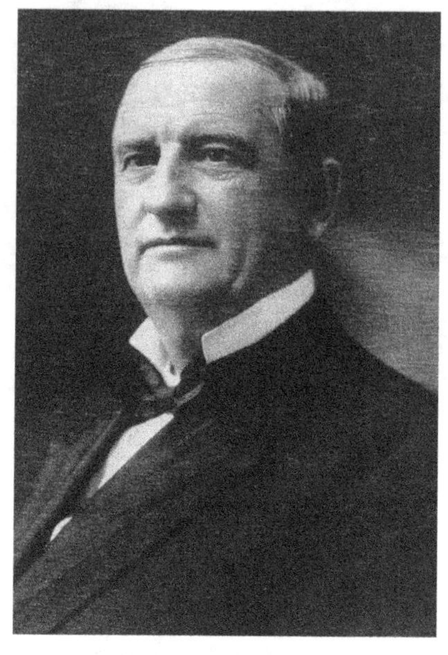

J.L. Caldwell built the city's first streetcar line and the Guyandotte Valley Railway. He and his partners organized the First National Bank of Huntington with Caldwell as president. *Marshall University Special Collections.*

In Guyandotte, Caldwell operated a small hardware business with his father-in-law, Nicholas Smith. The two men also busied themselves in the timber business, which at that time saw thousands of trees felled and then, at periods of high water, floated down the Guyandotte River to the Ohio. Nimble-footed loggers would be astride the makeshift rafts of logs, endeavoring to guide them and keep them moving freely without jamming. Frequently, they would have to jump from one moving log to another. It was difficult and dangerous work.

Local legend tells of how one day, an agitated Caldwell, safe on shore, loudly called out to his men on the logs, urging them to "ride 'em!" At that point, one logger is said to have come ashore and said, "Why don't you ride 'em, Mr. Caldwell?"

Presumably, that was an offer Caldwell thought best to refuse.

When rail tycoon Collis P. Huntington arrived on the scene and founded his new town of Huntington, Caldwell moved quickly to take advantage of the opportunities this presented. In 1884, he and several partners organized the First National Bank of Huntington. Caldwell became the bank's president, a post he would continue to hold until his death nearly forty years later.

In 1887, Caldwell and his wife moved from their home on Main Street in Guyandotte to a handsome new Queen Anne–style home built for them at Third Avenue and Twelfth Street, then a fashionable address in the rapidly growing Huntington.

In 1889, Caldwell had a rail route surveyed to the Logan coal fields and offered it to the Norfolk & Western Railway, which apparently gave it careful consideration but ultimately decided not to build there.

Undiscouraged, Caldwell himself organized the Guyandotte Valley Railway Company and, after extensive negotiations, came to terms with the Chesapeake & Ohio Railway in constructing and operating the line built first to Midkiff in Lincoln County and then beyond.

Caldwell and his various partners owned thousands of acres of timber and coal land in southern West Virginia.

He organized Huntington's Consolidated Light & Railway Company in 1892, later selling it to U.S. senator Johnson L. Camden of Parkersburg, who incorporated it into his Camden Interstate Railway Company.

Caldwell erected the Caldwell Building, one of Huntington's earliest business buildings, at Fourth Avenue and Ninth Street, and he largely financed construction of the Hotel Frederick, long the city's leading hotel. He played a key role in the creation of Central City, located just went of Huntington, and induced a number of industries to locate there.

In 1914, with Caldwell as president, the First National Bank built an impressive new twelve-story building at Fourth Avenue and Tenth Street. Later, after a 1924 merger with the Huntington National Bank, the newly created First Huntington National Bank constructed a major addition that extended the building all the way back to the alley. (Today, it takes a careful eye to detect where the original building stops and the addition begins.)

Caldwell was seventy-seven when he died of pneumonia. Friends and family said he had been in declining health for some time. His daily visits to his desk at the bank had become rare events.

In 1926, the Huntington Board of Park Commissioners voted to allow the Caldwell family to erect in Ritter Park a marble fountain honoring the late business leader. The fountain is said to have cost $20,000—quite a sum of money in that day. The memorial was located on the hill known as Gobbler's Knob, near the current park amphitheater. Over time, the memorial's isolated location made it a tempting target for vandals who carved their names and initials into its tall marble columns. Thieves carried off the floodlights that had been installed to illuminate it at night. The fountain itself, which had featured a constant stream of water, eventually stopped working.

In 1939, one of Caldwell's daughters, Ida Caldwell McFaddin of Beaumont, Texas, complained to the park board that on a visit to Huntington, she had been "shocked and hurt" to see the monument's sad state. She asked that it be repaired or torn down. Her request set off a long tug-of-war between the strong-willed McFaddin and the members of the park board, who apparently hoped that at some point she would simply go away. Instead, she continued to pepper the board with angry complaints. Finally, in 1945, the board had the memorial dismantled.

CARTER G. WOODSON

Dr. Carter G. Woodson, a graduate of Huntington's old all-black Douglass High School who went on to earn a PhD from Harvard University, is widely recognized as the "Father of Black History Month."

Woodson was born in 1875 in Buckingham County, Virginia. As jobs opened up in West Virginia's coal mines and railroads, many black families migrated across the mountains from Virginia. Young Woodson's family was among them. At age nineteen, he enrolled at Douglass High. He finished the four-year course in two years and then went on to earn a degree from Berea College in Kentucky. In 1900, he returned to Huntington and became principal at Douglass.

He earned another bachelor's degree and master's degree from the University of Chicago and in 1912 was the second black man to earn a PhD from Harvard. (William E.B. Du Bois was the first.) Later, he studied at the Sorbonne in Paris, taught English in the Philippines and was dean at what is now West Virginia State University.

In 1915, Woodson organized the Association for the Study of Negro Life, where he served as director, researcher, editor and janitor. The next year, he founded the influential *Journal of Negro History*. Today's observance of Black History Month can be traced directly to his pioneering efforts. He spent his later years in Washington, D.C., where he died in 1950.

Woodson's fame has grown over the years. In 1984, the U.S. Postal Service issued a stamp in his honor—a fitting tribute to him and his influential

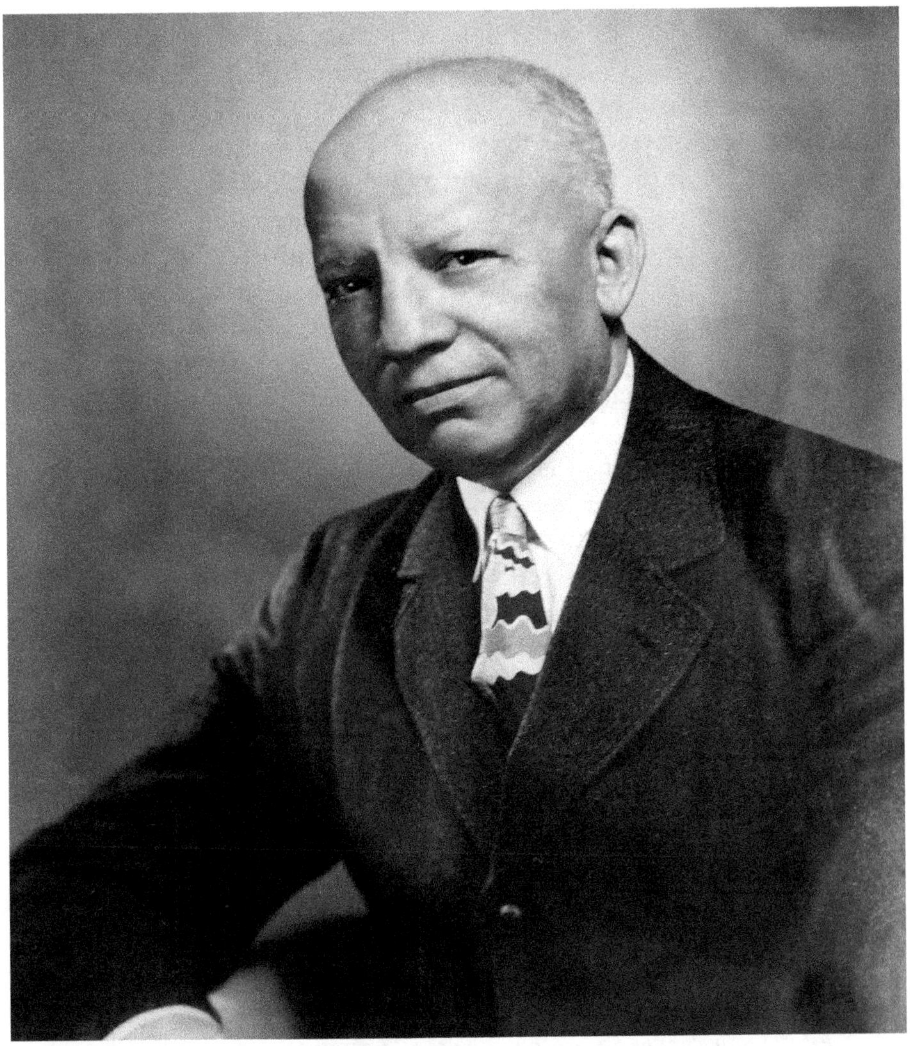

Dr. Carter G. Woodson, who received his early education in Huntington, is widely recognized as the "Father of Black History Month." *Library of Congress.*

legacy. Yet he long went virtually unremembered and unacknowledged in his adopted hometown of Huntington.

Today, fortunately, that has changed. A handsome statue of the famed black educator stands on the lawn of the Carter G. Woodson Apartments on Huntington's Hal Greer Boulevard. And the Woodson Memorial Foundation, which erected the statue in 1995, is continuing its efforts to keep his memory alive.

In a sense, Woodson's statue honors not just one man but the many black citizens whose vision and accomplishment helped build Huntington into the community it is today.

Black laborers played a major role in building the tracks of the C&O Railway that gave birth to Huntington and undoubtedly helped erect many of the city's first structures.

In the 1870s, the Reverend Nelson Barnett walked from Buckingham County, Virginia, to Huntington. Upon his arrival, he found a bustling town that clearly needed more workers. He returned to Virginia and brought back a wagonload of men to work for the C&O. Most of their names are lost to history, but we know that one of them was James Woodson—the father of Carter G. Woodson.

More blacks flocked to the new city, many of them finding work as waiters, cooks, bellmen for hotels, bartenders and orderlies in hospitals or private homes. Later came the first of the city's black ministers, doctors and businessmen—men such as the Reverend R.J. Perkins, Baptist minister; Dr. C.C. Barnett, a black physician; and Isaac Miller, who opened the city's first barbershop for blacks. Over Huntington's history, countless other black citizens have offered their unique contributions to the city's fabric of life. Many have gone on to prominence in state and national affairs.

Dr. W.K. Elliott, a Huntington dentist, longtime member of the Huntington Housing Authority and expert on the city's black history, put it well when, in 1971, he wrote:

> *It is a long journey from the chains of slavery to community and national leadership, but America's black man has made the trip, through seemingly insurmountable odds at times. The result of that journey is realized today as the black man is taking his place in city, state and national affairs. Like Huntington, he has reached a place of prominence—a rightful place, indeed.*

"COIN" HARVEY

William Hope Harvey (1851–1936), better known as "Coin" Harvey, was by turns a teacher, lawyer, silver miner, author, resort owner and presidential candidate. Most of his ventures were unsuccessful, except for his writing. Although mostly forgotten today, his *Coin's Financial School*, a pamphlet published in 1894, sold more than one million copies.

Born at Buffalo in Putnam County, West Virginia, William was the fifth of Robert and Anna Harvey's six children. At age sixteen, he tried his hand at teaching school but, dissatisfied, went on to read for the law and was admitted to the bar at nineteen. He practiced briefly in Barboursville, then moved to Huntington and went into practice with an older brother, Thomas.

The entire Harvey clan was now living in Huntington. Another brother, Harry, had bought a store in Huntington and, impressed by the growing town, had persuaded his father to move the family off the farm.

In 1874, seemingly intending to settle down in Huntington, William Harvey built a handsome house of his own design. He picked a choice Third Avenue lot where the best families of the day were building, and he came up with a design that was heavily influenced by the classic appearance of houses he had seen during a visit to New Orleans. As a result, his house looks vastly different from other Huntington houses built at about the same time.

The construction of the house was every bit as unusual as its appearance. Instead of a typical wood frame, the house was built much like a log cabin, but with thick stacks of wood planks substituting for the logs. The planks

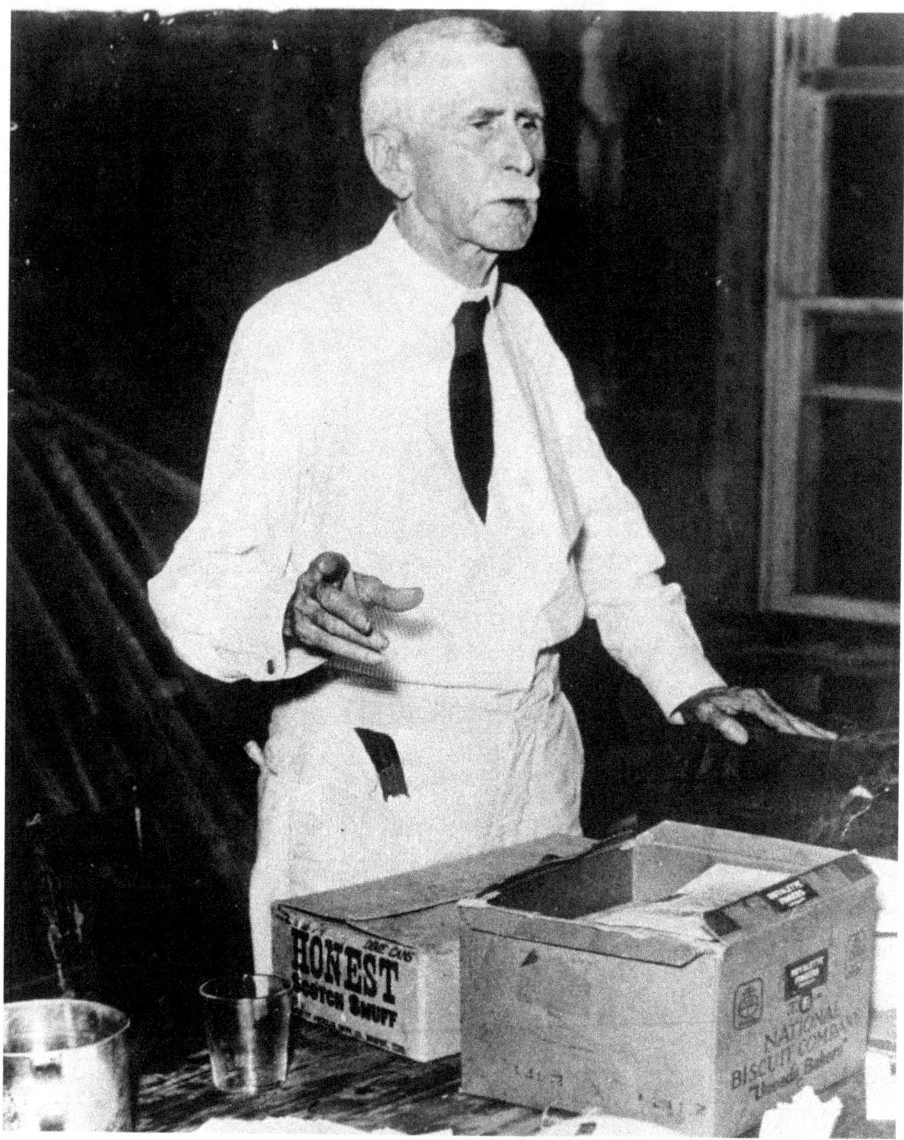

William Hope Harvey was the author of *Coin's Financial School*, an 1894 political pamphlet that sold more than one million copies during the "free silver" debate that then raged. *Author's collection.*

were fastened together with long spikes. Local legend says the stucco applied to the outside of the Harvey house was made from the first concrete mixed in Huntington.

One of the oldest surviving dwellings in the Huntington area, the Harvey house has been put to a number of uses over the years. It once housed a doctor's office and at one point was even home to a motorcycle club. It long stood vacant and neglected. In recent years, a private foundation headed by Huntington attorney James W. St. Clair and his wife, Mickey, has slowly worked to restore the historic house and preserve it for future generations to enjoy.

A report by Huntington architect Robert J. Summerfeldt, hired by St. Clair to evaluate the old house, concluded: "The unique character, design, location and history of this structure and its creator unquestionably qualify it for extraordinary efforts to restore and maintain its distinctive presence and history in the city of Huntington."

Ironically, it may be that Harvey never lived in the remarkable house he designed. Certainly, he couldn't have lived in it for very long, for the very next year after its construction, the restless lawyer moved to Gallipolis, Ohio, where he met and, in 1876, married Anna Halliday. The couple soon moved to Cleveland. In 1883, when Harvey went to Colorado on behalf of a client, he became interested in silver mining. The next year, he moved his family there and started working silver claims.

In Colorado, Harvey was introduced to the "free silver" political movement. Increased production and a decision by Congress to stop minting silver coins had combined to send the price of silver plunging. Harvey and other silver miners were the first to demand "free"—that is, unrestricted—silver coinage, but poor farmers in the South and West quickly took up the cause.

Returning to Chicago, Harvey began printing and selling by mail a series of pamphlets promoting the "free silver" cause. The first two pamphlets sold poorly, but the third—*Coin's Financial School*—was a phenomenal success. It purported to be an account of a school where a boy called only Professor Coin—the source, of course, of Harvey's nickname—painstakingly explains the superiority of silver coinage as opposed to gold. Harvey gave his little paperbound volume such an air of authenticity that many readers were convinced the school and Professor Coin were real.

Harvey's widely read pamphlet was instrumental in aiding William Jennings Bryan's 1896 presidential campaign. That year saw Bryan capture the Democratic nomination for president by stampeding the party's Chicago convention with his oratory. "You shall not crucify mankind upon a cross of gold!" he thundered. Bryan, of course, lost to William McKinley that year, and although he tried for the White House again in 1900 and 1908, "free silver" was by then a dead issue.

An embittered Harvey abandoned Chicago for Arkansas, where he opened a mountain resort. Initially successful, the Mount Ne resort soon fell on hard times. Harvey, convinced that civilization was on the verge of collapse, embarked on building a giant pyramid intended to house the history of mankind's rise and fall. Only the amphitheater planned for the pyramid's base was built. In 1932, Liberty Party delegates from twenty-six states met in the amphitheater and nominated the eighty-year-old Harvey for president. Even though he did no campaigning, he received more than fifty thousand votes.

In 1936, Coin Harvey died proud but penniless. The Mount Ne resort had to be sold to pay his debts.

SAM GIDEON

Sam Gideon (1836–1923) was one of Huntington's earliest merchants and most prominent citizens. "Uncle Sam," as he was known to his many customers and friends, was short in stature—standing only five feet, seven inches, tall—but nevertheless cast a huge shadow over the young city's daily affairs.

Born at Württemberg in Germany, Gideon came to this country in 1854 without a penny to his name. Even though he knew only a few words of English, he somehow managed to make his way to Rock Island, Illinois, where a family friend took him in.

While in Illinois, Gideon was in the audience for one of the famed 1858 debates between Abraham Lincoln (a Republican) and Stephen A. Douglas (a Democrat), who were battling each other for an Illinois seat in the U.S. Senate. At that time, state legislatures elected senators. The debates presaged Lincoln's successful 1860 presidential campaign and are remembered for the considerable eloquence with which both men presented their arguments. Practically the only issue discussed was slavery.

Gideon became an ardent Lincoln supporter. When the Confederates fired on Fort Sumter and Lincoln called for volunteers to suppress the rebellion, Gideon was one of the first to answer the president's call. Enlisting in the Twenty-Seventh Illinois Volunteer Infantry, Gideon served in the Union army for three years and fought in a number of major battles, including Chickamauga. He emerged from the war as a lieutenant.

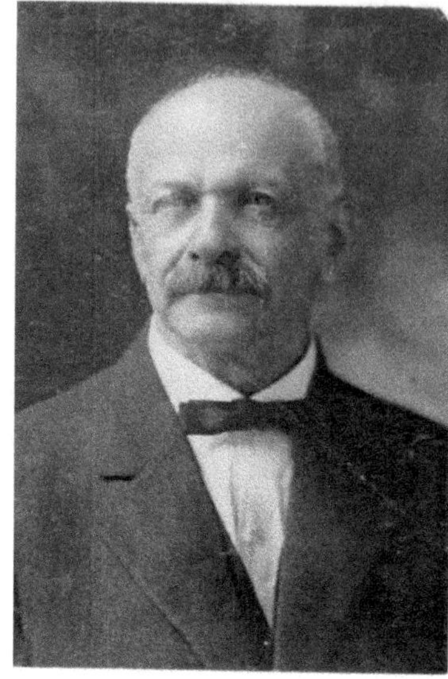

German-born Sam Gideon operated a Huntington clothing store that was a busy part of the city's retail scene for more than fifty years. *Marshall University Special Collections.*

At the war's end, Gideon moved to Cincinnati, Ohio, where, in 1865, he married Dora Epopinger. Like her husband, she had come to this country from Germany. The young couple moved from Cincinnati to Manchester and then, in 1872, to Huntington, where they would live for the rest of their lives.

Within a month of his arrival in Huntington, Gideon opened a clothing store at 949 Third Avenue. The store would be a busy part of the city's retail scene for more than fifty years. Initially, Gideon and his wife lived upstairs over the store, but later they moved to a home in the 400 block of Thirteenth Avenue on the city's South Side.

Gideon's first foray into local politics came in 1876, when he won election to Huntington City Council. Four years later, he unsuccessfully ran for mayor against Dr. E.S. Buffington, a son of the city's first mayor, Peter Cline Buffington. Gideon was reelected to council in 1886 and the next year played a major role in establishing the city's first water system.

A member of the Huntington Board of Education for nearly twenty-five years, Gideon also served on the Cabell County Court and was president of the court when the courthouse was completed in 1901.

Gideon helped found the first Jewish congregation in Huntington, was one of the organizers of the local Odd Fellows Lodge and served as commander of the Huntington post of the Grand Army of the Republic, the organization of Union army veterans.

With the death of his wife early in 1923, Gideon's health began to fail, and he died four months later, on June 20 of that year. Describing his funeral, the *Herald-Dispatch* wrote: "Hundreds of Huntington's most prominent men and women mingled with men and women of all classes, races and religious beliefs to pay tribute to one of the city's pioneers."

Rabbi A. Feinstein, who conducted the services, labeled Gideon a saint. "Judaism does not worship saints but it reveres and loves them," the rabbi told the assembled mourners. "Such a man was the late Sam Gideon. We are met here to revere the memory of a saint. Everyone knew Sam as one of the best citizens in the community and everyone recognized in him only the best."

In 1928, the Cabell County Court honored Gideon by naming one of the county's magisterial districts after him.

Sam and Dora Gideon had six children. Their oldest son, Dave (1873–1950), would, like his father, play an outsized role in the city's affairs. Born upstairs over the family clothing store, Dave would go on to become a clerk in the store and later his father's partner. After his father's death, he sold the business.

In 1913, Dave bought a part interest in the *Herald-Dispatch* and in 1920 was named the newspaper's publisher. Later, the *Advertiser* and the *Herald-Dispatch* merged to form the Huntington Publishing Company, and in 1936, he became president of the merged company, a position he held until his death.

Active behind the scenes in Republican politics for many years, Dave Gideon served as a respected informal adviser to many political figures on the local, state and national levels.

RUFUS SWITZER

Rufus Switzer (1855–1947) was a lawyer, banker, businessman and political figure who twice served as mayor of Huntington. On his death, he left a remarkable legacy.

His father, Jonathan Switzer, taught before the Civil War at Howell's Mill in rural Cabell County. In his *Cabell County Annals and Families*, local historian George S. Wallace described the elder Switzer as a "scholarly gentleman, splendid teacher, a leader in the community…[who] had the power of making friends of all in his large circle of acquaintances."

Young Rufus apparently inherited many of his father's fine qualities. He attended Marshall College, briefly taught school and then studied law at the University of Virginia, graduating in 1881. He began practicing law in Putnam County, where he was elected to serve in the State Senate, his first foray into politics. He moved to Huntington in 1891 and immediately involved himself in politics, winning election to city council. He was elected mayor in 1909.

The year before Switzer became mayor, the city had purchased a tract of land along Four Pole Creek as the site for an incinerator. Not surprisingly, some of the site's neighbors objected, and a real donnybrook ensued. As mayor, Switzer settled the matter by declaring that the purchased property would become a park—the city's first ever. Although Switzer was the driving force behind the park, it was named Ritter Park when businessman C.L. Ritter donated two tracts of land that significantly enlarged it.

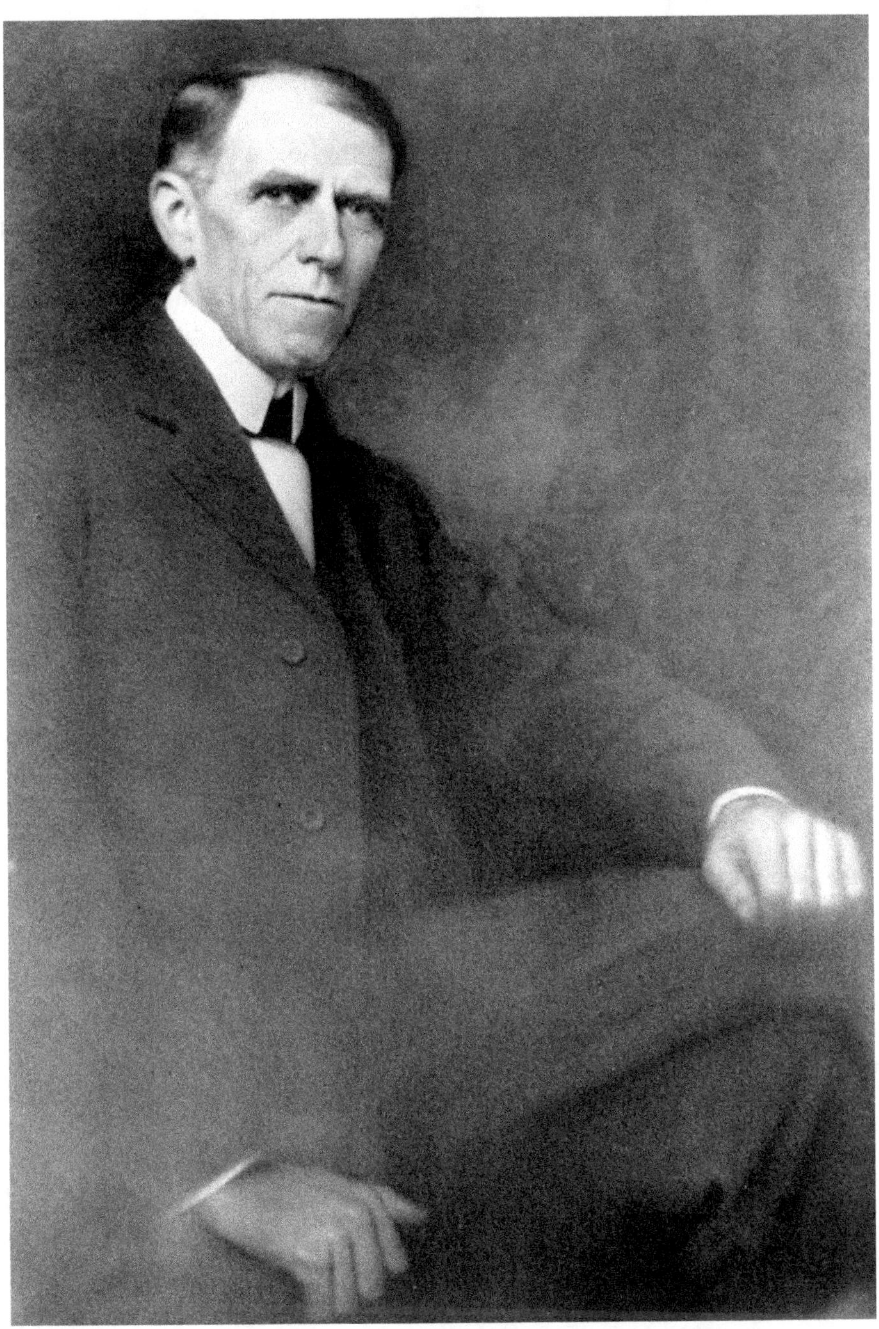

Although it was ultimately named for businessman C.L. Ritter, Mayor Rufus Switzer was the architect of the deal that created Ritter Park, enjoyed by generations of Huntingtonians. *Herald-Dispatch*.

It was also during Switzer's first term as mayor that residents in Guyandotte and Central City, then independent communities, were persuaded to be annexed into Huntington. He served as mayor until 1912 and then was appointed to the post again in 1918 to fill the unexpired term of Mayor Leon S. Wiles, who fell victim to that year's influenza epidemic.

Contemporaries described Switzer as a tall man with a lively sense of humor. His driving interest in life, it's said, was the betterment of the community. From the 1920s to the 1940s, he was active as a lawyer, banker and real estate developer. In his Cabell County history, Wallace described him as "one of the builders of Huntington."

Switzer was ninety-one when he died in 1947, but his influence remains very much alive today. In his will, he established a perpetual trust and directed that two-thirds of the annual net income from that trust go "for the use and maintenance of an art gallery, historical museum and cultural center, for the development of the character and interest of the children and other citizens of Huntington, Cabell County and West Virginia."

In the Huntington Museum of Art (HMA)'s formative years, Switzer's generous bequest was literally the lifeblood of the institution. From its modest beginnings in the 1950s, HMA has grown into one of the nation's finest small museums, and it continues to benefit from Switzer's vision and generosity.

Switzer directed that the other third of the net income from his trust go "for the study, research and treatment of human disease." The Huntington Clinical Foundation Inc. was organized to carry out the terms of Switzer's bequest and each year distributes thousands of dollars to a long list of medical and healthcare projects.

A popular park, a thriving museum, a healthier community—that's the legacy of Rufus Switzer.

JOSEPH H. LONG

As a schoolboy growing up in Pittsburgh, Joseph Harvey Long (1863–1958) had a little hand press and by the time he was twelve years old had established a thriving business printing calling cards, handbills and the like. By age eighteen, he was working twelve hours a day as a newspaper typesetter. Later, he worked as a printer on various papers in Pennsylvania, Ohio, New York and West Virginia. In Wheeling, West Virginia, he and a partner, H.G. Ogden, bought an all-but-defunct paper, renamed it the *Wheeling News* and turned it into a modest success. But Long was determined to run his own paper.

Hearing that a paper was for sale in Huntington, Long investigated and in 1893 purchased the *Huntington Herald.* At the same time, he sold his interest in the *Wheeling News* to Ogden.

The match between the *Herald* and its new owner was a difficult one. Newspapers of that era were intensely political. Long was a lifelong Democrat; the *Herald* was a Republican paper. So he soon sold it and acquired the *Huntington Advertiser*, a small daily whose politics matched his own. It became the first building block in what would become a local media empire.

In 1901, Long purchased property in the 900 block of Fourth Avenue, where the Keith-Albee Theater now stands, and built there what was then the most modern newspaper plant in West Virginia.

Meanwhile, the *Herald* had merged with the *Huntington Dispatch* to become the *Herald-Dispatch.* For a number of years, Long's afternoon *Advertiser*

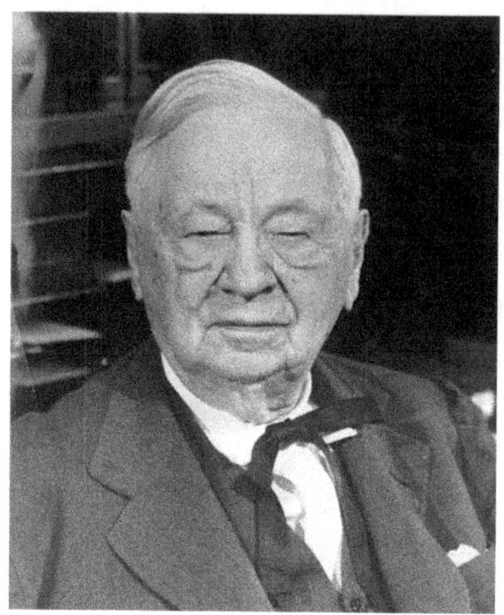

In 1895, Joseph Harvey Long acquired the *Huntington Advertiser*, the first building block in what would become a local media empire. *Herald-Dispatch.*

slugged it out with the morning *Herald-Dispatch*, owned by Dave Gideon. In 1924, Colonel Long (the title was strictly honorary, bestowed by Governor William Glasscock) bought the northwest corner of Fifth Avenue and Tenth Street and erected a new building for his paper. Not be outdone, the *Herald-Dispatch* built a new home just a few doors down.

Shortly thereafter, the two rival newspapers declared a truce and merged as the Huntington Publishing Company, with Long as chairman and Gideon as president. The *Herald-Dispatch* abandoned its new building and moved into the *Advertiser* building. The papers' mechanical and business operations were combined while the two news staffs remained separate and highly competitive. Both Long and Gideon remained publishers of their respective newspapers until their deaths.

The Huntington Publishing Company also purchased the state's oldest radio station, WSAZ, and in 1949 started one of the nation's first television stations, WSAZ-TV, Channel 3.

His newspaper and broadcast accomplishments would have earned Long his full due in any history of Huntington. But from his earliest days in Huntington, he was an active community leader. He was Huntington's postmaster from 1916 to 1921. Elected president of the Huntington Chamber of Commerce in 1936, he was reelected for four consecutive years.

In the wake of the disastrous 1937 Ohio River flood, he reached into his own pocket to help those newspaper employees who suffered lost or damaged homes, and he then played a key role in the successful effort to see a floodwall constructed that would protect the city against future floods.

In 1938, he led the campaign that convinced Cabell County voters to approve a $1.5 million school bond, which enabled construction of Huntington East High School.

He was a director of the First Huntington National Bank, the Huntington-Ohio Bridge Company, the Ohio Valley Bus Company and the Morris

Memorial Hospital in Milton. He was treasurer of the First Congregational Church for more than thirty years.

Long was a generous supporter of what was then Marshall College, maintaining especially close ties with the school's journalism department. He was also a friend of the arts. He served on the board of the Huntington Symphony Association and was a lifelong board member of the Huntington Galleries, now the Huntington Museum of Art.

He remained active until shortly before his death—at age ninety-one—on December 29, 1958.

HERMAN P. DEAN

Herman P. Dean, who died in 1978 at the age of eighty, packed several lifetimes of experiences into his busy eight decades.

A businessman, Dean owned Huntington's former Standard Printing and Publishing Company, as well as other firms. A newspaperman, he was publisher of the *Wayne County News.* A church and civic leader, he taught a Sunday school class at Huntington's Central Christian Church for thirty years and generously supported a long list of charitable endeavors. A world traveler, he visited not just the familiar foreign ports of call but such isolated regions as Canada's Yukon Territory and Hudson's Bay. He even lived with the Eskimos for two years.

Dean loved hunting, fishing and collecting antique guns. He spent a lifetime amassing his collection and then presented it to the Huntington Museum of Art for future generations to admire and enjoy. Today, the Herman P. Dean Firearms Collection is one of the museum's most popular exhibits. The Dean Collection numbers four hundred items and traces the historical development of arms from the fourteenth-century crossbow and early "hand cannon" to the weaponry of the mid-twentieth century. The collection includes one of frontiersman Daniel Boone's Kentucky rifles, a Winchester rifle owned by a member of the Hatfield clan during the legendary Hatfield-McCoy feud and a pistol said to have been used in the 1875 holdup of the Bank of Huntington.

Born at Wayne on May 6, 1897, Dean learned as a boy to love the outdoors. In later years, when he wasn't off globe-trotting, he lived on a

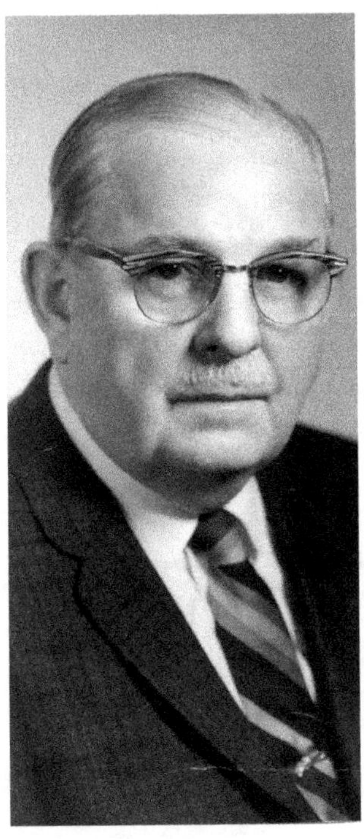

Nationally known gun expert Herman P. Dean donated his antique firearms collection to the Huntington Museum of Art, where it remains a popular exhibit. *Huntington Museum of Art.*

thirty-five-acre tract on Twelve Pole Creek in Wayne County just outside Huntington. In 1973, he told an interviewer that he had shot "just about every animal in North America," including a 1,650-pound Kodiak bear.

Like many other sportsmen, he became increasingly interested in conservation. "I get more fun out of restocking and conservation than I did formerly out of fishing and shooting game," he said. "I now raise a great deal more game than I kill."

Given his love of hunting, it's perhaps not surprising that Dean would begin collecting guns. Once he did, he found himself fascinated not only with the craftsmanship that went into the weapons but also with the history they had to tell.

"The history of the world," he once said, "parallels firearms developments. I like guns from the standpoints of historical significance, art, mechanical progress and ingenuity. And I enjoy the friendship of men who love guns.... Then, too, it's a hobby that fits in with advancing years, for the time does come in life when it is hard to follow a pack of blooded 'coon hounds over the mountains of West Virginia."

Over the years, Dean became a nationally recognized authority on firearms. His articles were widely published in magazines. And although his Standard Printing and Publishing was primarily a commercial printing operation, not a book publisher, he nevertheless used the company to publish a whole shelf of books about guns, some of which he wrote and some written by other gun experts. Many were printed in limited editions, making them now valuable and eagerly sought by collectors.

Typical of the relationship Dean saw between guns and history was the interest he developed in Daniel Boone.

> *I didn't know much about the history of West Virginia until I started collecting guns and found out that Daniel Boone was at one time an inhabitant of the Kanawha Valley. I happened to be fortunate enough to*

> *come across one of his guns and a beaver trap that he owned and I got to studying Boone, got everything I could on him, and to me it opened the door of my own state's history.*

Dean sold his business interests and retired in 1961 but certainly didn't take to his rocker. He established an office in a downtown bank building and there—surrounded by Eskimo art, tusks of ivory and a world globe—he busied himself writing magazine articles and letters to his many friends scattered around the world. In addition, he enjoyed teaching the museum's volunteer guides about his collection and sometimes personally conducted tours for visiting groups.

In the final years of his life, Dean liked to point out that he no longer owned a single gun. What he didn't donate to the Huntington Museum of Art, he gave to other institutions or to friends. Afterward, he said, "I didn't feel particularly bad when I gave them away and saw people enjoying viewing them as much as I enjoyed collecting them."

MEMPHIS TENNESSEE GARRISON

On a cold winter day in the early 1900s, a young African American girl decided she was tired of sitting in the segregated Jim Crow car of the train she was riding. With no heat, the car was little warmer than the frigid temperature outside. So she got up and moved to one of the train's other cars kept warm by a pot-bellied stove. Taking a seat, she soon fell asleep.

In an interview more than seventy years later, she recalled what happened next. Making his way through the train, the conductor spotted the girl and shook her awake.

"Go along to the other coach," he angrily demanded.

"Where?" the girl asked.

"In there," he said, pointing to the car she had left.

"It's cold in there," she said, reluctantly doing as she was told.

Then and there, the girl decided that when she grew up, she would be a lawyer and make the world a better place, changing things like the ugly Jim Crow laws of that era.

Memphis Tennessee Garrison didn't become a lawyer. ("My mother couldn't wash enough clothes to send me to law school.") But change things she did, as a schoolteacher and nationally known civil rights worker.

The daughter and granddaughter of freed slaves, she was born in Hollins, Virginia, in 1890 and named after an aunt who was a teacher in Memphis. "My mother had never been to Biloxi, Mississippi; otherwise I might have had that name."

As a young girl, she lived in Gary, in McDowell County, West Virginia, where her father worked as a coal miner and her mother washed clothes at the mine superintendent's house. Life was hard and got even harder when the young girl's father was killed in a railroad accident.

The girl understood her heritage early. She touched the scars on her grandfather's back, left from a slave driver's whip. "The welts on Granddaddy's back were like your finger ridges, crisscrossed just as that whip struck."

Her strong-willed mother was determined that her daughter, an avid reader from an early age, would get an education. So she was sent to Columbus, Ohio, to live with a family there while attending high school. Later, she studied at Ohio University and West Virginia State College and graduated from Bluefield State College. Diploma in hand, she was hired as a teacher in Gary.

On her first day on the job, she found there were no books for her class, so she used Sears, Roebuck catalogues to teach her students how to read. In an era long before schools started breakfast programs, she dug into her own pocket to provide hot breakfasts for her pupils.

She taught school in the McDowell County coal fields for more than forty years. During her years in the classroom, she touched the lives of thousands of students—and personally paid to send some of them on to college.

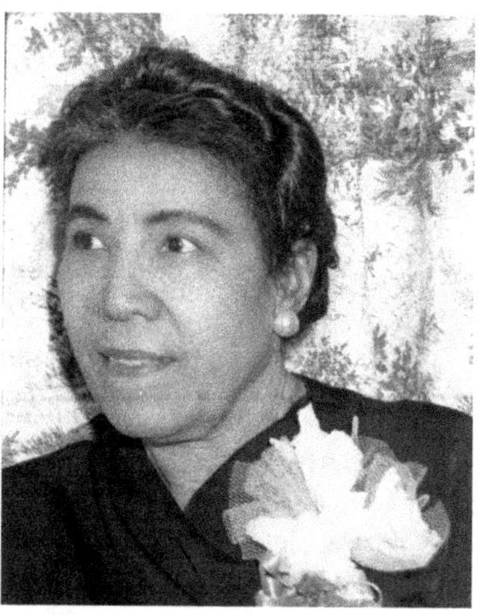

Teacher and civil rights worker Memphis Tennessee Garrison helped organize NAACP chapters throughout West Virginia and rose in the NAACP ranks to become a national vice president. *Herald-Dispatch.*

But her influence would be felt far beyond her classroom.

She was the first woman president of the West Virginia State Teachers Association and served as vice president of the American Teachers Association. She helped organize NAACP chapters throughout West Virginia and rose in the NAACP ranks to become a national vice president. She began a Negro Artists Series, which brought nationally recognized entertainers and speakers to the coal fields. She helped create a recreation center with a swimming pool and picnic grounds. Frequently, she was called on as a mediator, helping resolve differences between U.S. Steel, the company that owned the mines at Gary, and its workforce.

In the 1950s, she retired and moved to Huntington. But retirement didn't stop her from battling for the causes she believed in.

Garrison had been a Girl Scout leader in Gary. Arriving in Huntington, she found there was no Scout troop for black girls. So she started one. Later, when she met an educator from Nigeria who talked of his country's desperate need for books, she embarked on a one-woman book drive that saw more than 1,500 books shipped to Nigeria. In 1969, she organized a drive that sent thousands of dollars in food aid to hungry black children in Mississippi.

From 1963 to 1966, Garrison was a member of the first West Virginia Human Rights Commission. In 1970, Marshall University awarded her an honorary doctorate of humanities degree.

Memphis Tennessee Garrison died in 1988. She was ninety-eight years old.

STEWART H. SMITH

In a sense, Marshall University's history can be divided into two parts—everything before 1961 and everything since.

It was in 1961 that the West Virginia legislature approved a measure making a reality of Marshall's long-cherished dream of becoming a university. Moving up to university status laid the foundation for the spectacular growth that has unfolded at Marshall in recent years.

That historic victory was truly a team effort. But while the team had many players, it had only one coach: a determined President Stewart H. Smith, who literally worked night and day to win over reluctant state lawmakers and convince them that Marshall merited the elevated status it was seeking. Popular with students, faculty and the community, Smith served as Marshall's president for more than two decades, longer than any of Marshall's other presidents before or since.

A native of York, Pennsylvania, Smith was a graduate of Gettysburg College, where he was an English major and president of the student body. He later earned a master's degree from Columbia and a doctorate in education at Syracuse University. Before coming to Marshall, he taught English in the public schools, served as a high school principal and was a faculty member at Syracuse.

Smith was dean of the Marshall Teachers College in the summer of 1946, when John D. Williams resigned as Marshall president. The West Virginia Board of Education, which then administered the state's colleges, appointed Smith interim president and at the end of the 1946–47 school year made that temporary appointment permanent.

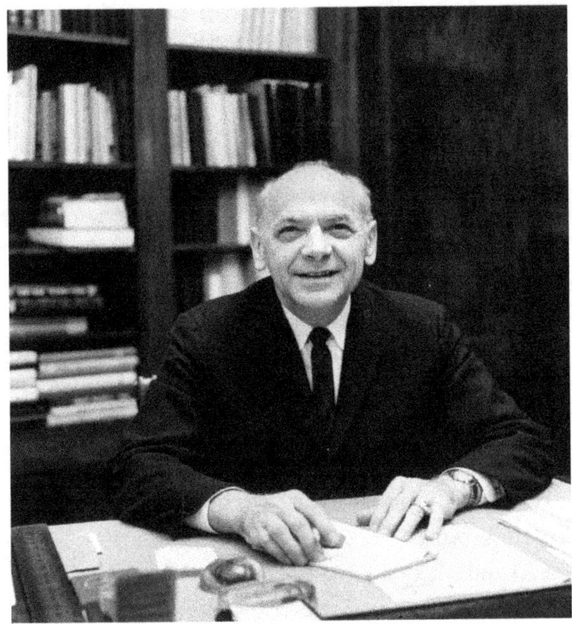

Popular with Marshall faculty, students and the community, Dr. Stewart H. Smith headed the school for twenty-two years, longer than any other Marshall president before or since. *Marshall University Special Collections.*

During Smith's years as president, Marshall's enrollment mushroomed from 3,500 students to 8,500, eight major buildings were erected and the school's course offerings greatly expanded. But it was the attainment of university status that stands as his greatest achievement.

As early as 1927, the Marshall Alumni Association went on record favoring university status for Marshall College. No one took the suggestion seriously at the time, and the 1930s and 1940s, with the Great Depression and World War II, were hardly appropriate years for such an ambitious move. But with the war's end and enactment of the GI Bill, returning veterans swelled Marshall's enrollment and started people seriously talking about Marshall as a university. In 1957, the North Central Association, the regional accrediting body for higher education, officially classified Marshall as a "university type institution."

In 1960, Smith asked the state board of education to designate Marshall a university, telling the board: "Unbiased observers…will be quick to recognize that it is only through the formal designation of Marshall as a university that the institution…can occupy its vital role in the future of higher education in our state."

The board refused Smith's request. But the next year, 1961, it reconsidered and recommended that the legislature designate Marshall a university. That's when the real fight began. The board's recommendation touched off a no-holds-barred legislative battle between Marshall's backers and supporters of West Virginia University, who were determined to preserve its status as the state's only university.

A Morgantown newspaper editorially denounced Marshall's "fever of empire building." WVU's immediate past president, Elvis Starr, then secretary of the army, proclaimed that Marshall ought to dedicate itself to being "a first-rate college, rather a fourth-rate university." The extent of the WVU supporters' opposition, Smith later suggested, may have alienated some legislators "who might otherwise have opposed us."

In his campus history, *Marshall University: An Institution Comes of Age*, Dr. Charles Moffat, the school's legendary history professor, labels Smith "an articulate and indefatigable spokesman for the partisans of Marshall College." In that role, Smith logged literally thousands of miles on West Virginia's highways and back roads, driving to every corner of the state to personally talk with legislators, newspaper editors and countless others he thought might be willing to aid Marshall's cause.

Finally, when the smoke of battle cleared and the votes were counted, the State Senate approved the Marshall bill on February 16, 1961, and four days later, the House of Delegates followed suit. Governor W.W. Barron already had said he would sign the bill; thus, it was clear Marshall had won.

At the time, some legislative insiders claimed one reason for Marshall's victory was a bit of old-fashioned vote trading between lawmakers from the state's northern and southern counties. Northern legislators working to gain passage of a constitutional amendment legalizing "liquor by the drink" in West Virginia are said to have agreed to support the Marshall bill in exchange for southern legislators' agreeing to vote for the booze bill. At this point, a half century later, it's impossible to say just how big a factor this might have been in the passage of both measures.

When the news of the legislature's approval of the Marshall bill reached Huntington, it set off impromptu campus celebrations, which saw students shouting with glee and waving copies of an extra published by *The Parthenon*, the campus newspaper. The newspaper's huge headline: "We Are Now Marshall U."

Here's Smith's own description of that day:

> *I was in my office and didn't know the Legislature had passed it. All at once we heard a terrific roar coming across campus. Hundreds of students... came to Old Main. They called me out and asked me to make a speech....I couldn't talk; I couldn't form a word. I guess I finally said something.*

> *We had worked so hard. We had almost given up getting it through the Legislature. Then to have it happen was such an emotional shock.*

On March 2, Governor Barron visited the campus to sign the bill into law, saying, "It is my sincere wish that Marshall's future will be resplendent with new pride and progress."

Indeed, "pride and progress" may be said to have been the hallmarks of Stewart Smith's years as Marshall's president. He retired in 1968. Rather than return to his native Pennsylvania, Smith chose to remain in Huntington. He died in 1982 at age seventy-eight.

WALTER W. PAYNE

Many of Huntington's mayors over the years have faded into relative obscurity. Not Walter W. Payne, surely one of the most colorful mayors in the city's history.

In the 1930s and '40s, New York City mayor Fiorello La Guardia's boundless energy and enthusiasm made him a nationally known—and immensely popular—figure. Often called the "Little Flower," the English translation of his Italian first name, La Guardia was elected New York mayor in 1934 and was twice reelected before deciding in 1945 that he wouldn't run again.

A bit more than a decade later, Huntingtonians would enjoy applying the same nickname to one of their own mayors: W.W. Payne.

Payne, who served as Huntington's mayor from 1949 to 1952, not only exhibited the same brand of energy and enthusiasm as La Guardia, but he also was built along much the same lines. Both were short in stature and stocky in build. The comparison with the popular New York mayor was obvious.

He hated sitting behind his desk at city hall. He loved to get out of the office and move around. With his seemingly limitless store of energy, he loved to be in the thick of things, whether it was a late-night debate at city hall or a three-alarm fire somewhere.

As mayor, he felt a special kinship with the Huntington Fire Department. He frequently donned the heavy coat, rubber boots and distinctive helmet of a fireman and chased the fire trucks to the scene of a blaze. At the fire,

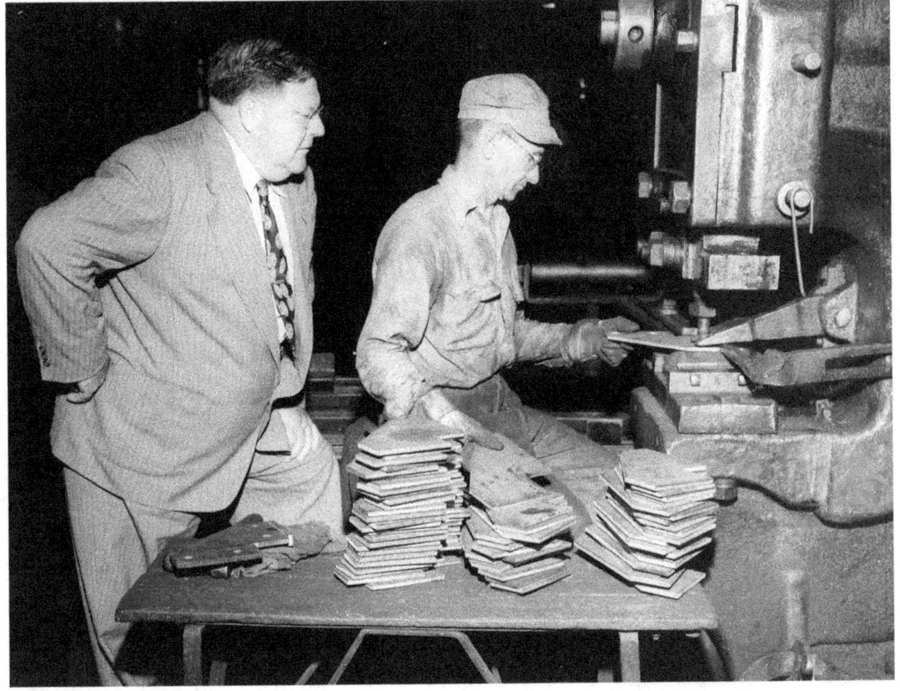

Mayor Walter W. Payne hated being confined to his city hall office, escaping whenever he could. Here, he's shown during a visit to Huntington's ACF railcar plant. *Herald-Dispatch.*

he generally confined himself to crowd control but more than once was known to bark a command when he thought a fireman wasn't doing what he thought needed to be done.

Payne's father and grandfather before him were in the milling business in Columbus, Ohio, and as a young man, the future mayor traveled much of the United States as a salesman for a milling company. Coming to Huntington in 1910, he opened a feed store on West Fourteenth Street, which he successfully operated until he retired in 1948.

Payne had planned to spend his retirement years hunting and fishing, but he was persuaded to run for mayor instead. He had never sought political office before but had been active in civic affairs. He was president of the Huntington Chamber of Commerce in 1930 and headed the Huntington Rotary Club from 1928 to 1931. He was an Elk, a Red Man, a Mason, a Shriner and a member of the Huntington Chapter of United Commercial Travelers. He served on the county draft board during World War II and was a member of the Huntington Fire Civil Service Commission for ten years.

In addition to his passion for fire trucks, Payne had a lifelong love of the circus. He belonged to the Circus Fans Association of the World and often attended its national conventions.

When his wife, Henrietta, became interested in the national Boys Club organization, she convinced him to enlist a number of the city's leading businessmen to form Huntington's first Boys and Girls Club. When he sold his feed business to a national firm, he donated his brick store building to the club, which still occupies it. It's named in Henrietta Payne's honor.

Payne had little in the way of formal education but more than made up for that by, as an adult, undertaking a broad program of reading, including philosophy and psychology. He was a talented raconteur with a seemingly endless supply of stories, some of which he had picked up while traveling the country and others shared with him by his circus friends.

After he left office as mayor, Payne worked in the 1950s as the unpaid director of the county's Civil Defense program, an important endeavor in a time when school pupils were being taught to "duck and cover" and some homeowners were building bomb shelters in their basements or backyards.

He was one of Huntington's last elected mayors before the city's 1957 switch to a council-manager form of government, with appointed mayors performing only ceremonial duties. (The voters ordered a switch back to a strong mayor system in 1985.)

W.W. Payne died in 1961 at age eighty-one. On his death, the *Advertiser* eulogized him as one of Huntington's "most colorful, most entertaining, most respected and most widely known citizens."

Today, he is remembered not as a mayor who built big buildings or accomplished great political feats but as a man who loved life and his adopted hometown and did his best to kindle that same kind of appreciation in the hearts and minds of his fellow citizens.

HAROLD FRANKEL

Even though Harold Frankel spent the last twenty years of his life in Florida, Huntington has never forgotten his trademark grin and the seemingly boundless energy, enthusiasm and optimism he threw into everything he did. And those who knew him best say he never forgot Huntington.

Frankel is remembered for his accomplishments in both business and politics.

In business, Frankel took over operation of his father's clothing store, branched out into the appliance business, established a highly successful Holiday Inn on U.S. 60 East and then invested everything he had—and everything he could borrow—in construction of a new downtown hotel, the first built in the city in decades. The hotel has had its share of ups and downs over the years but remains a visible testimony to Frankel's faith in the city's future.

In politics, he was a member of Huntington City Council for a remarkable sixteen years, served four one-year terms as mayor under the city's former council-manager form of government and was Cabell County sheriff for four years. As mayor, the always-colorful Frankel delighted in the ceremonial aspects of the post. No politician, sports figure or other celebrity could quietly slip into town if Frankel knew he or she was coming, He picked them up at the airport, stuffed them into the backseat of his Lincoln convertible and carted them off to town in an impromptu parade, complete with a police escort, sirens blaring.

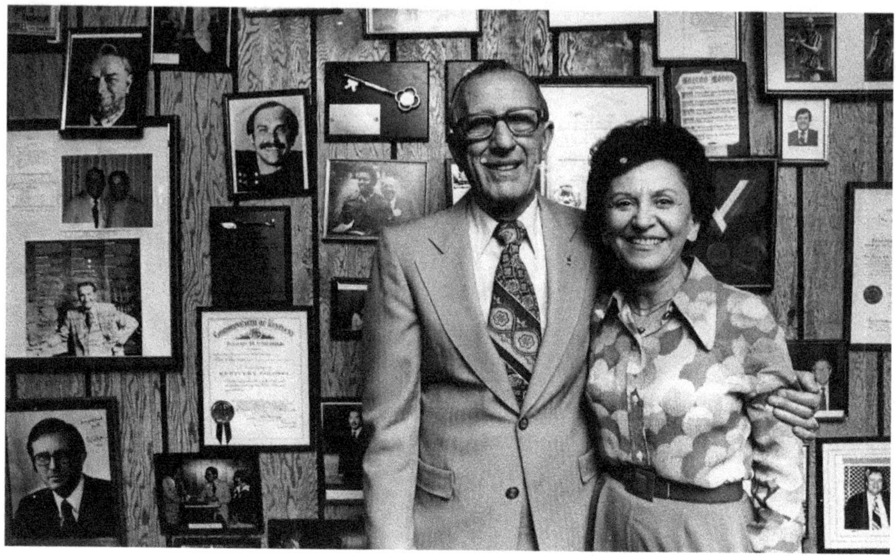

A familiar figure in both business and politics, Harold Frankel built the Holiday Inn, the city's first new downtown hotel in decades. With him is his wife, Dodi, his partner in everything he did. *Herald-Dispatch.*

Previous sheriffs had been perfectly content to wear a coat and tie like any businessman. Not Frankel. Once he was elected sheriff, he ordered himself a fancy white uniform with enough gold braid to gladden the heart of a South American dictator.

Veteran Huntington sports columnist Ernie Salvatore was Frankel's longtime friend. Here's Salvatore, his tongue only slightly tucked in his cheek, describing Frankel's arrival at a local sporting event:

> *Harold's grand entrances...were as colorful as they were impeccably timed. Dwindling minutes before an opening kickoff, tip off, starting gun or a boxing bout, there he'd come, dressed in a tailored getup, or casuals, sometimes wearing a big white hat with two holstered six shooters he couldn't hit the floor with, strapped to his sides. Now he was the Sheriff of Cabell County on a one-man parade. Without a horse. Striding the sidelines, in full view of everyone, waving to friends, real or imagined. A ready smile. Hands outstretched. The consummate actor, doing quite an act.*

The flamboyant Frankel had a serious side. Under the council-manager form of government, the mayor had no more power than any other city council member. Nonetheless, Frankel threw himself into the job.

Former city clerk Mary Neely recalls: "He would go through the city early in the morning and take notes about trash in the alley and things that needed fixing. He would give me the notes and tell me if I got them typed up by noon, he would buy me lunch. He was a wonderful man."

It's hard to name a civic group Frankel wasn't part of. He was on the board at Cammack Children's Center for thirty-eight years and the St. Mary's Hospital board for thirty-six years. He was president of the West Virginia League of Municipalities and the West Virginia Sheriffs' Association. Over the years, he helped raise untold thousands of dollars for the United Way, the Red Cross, the Cabell County Cancer Society, the Huntington YMCA, the March of Dimes and a host of other causes. Proud of his religious heritage, Frankel served Ohev Sholom Congregation in a number of posts.

The outgoing Frankel was a natural-born salesman—and when he opened the Holiday Inn on U.S. 60, he quickly demonstrated that he was just as adept at selling hotel rooms as he had been at selling clothes and appliances. In addition, Harold and his wife, Dodi, his partner in both marriage and business, made the hotel's Polynesian-style supper club, the Makiki, a highly popular local nightspot.

With the advent of the city's downtown urban renewal project, Frankel saw an opportunity to build a second Holiday Inn. He selected the same Third Avenue site where his father's store had once stood and set to work with his characteristic energy and optimism, but what he envisioned as a source of civic pride soon became a financial nightmare. Midway through construction, work came to a halt when the hotel's contractor went bankrupt. Next came a flurry of lawsuits between Frankel, other investors and the insurance company that wrote the construction bond on the project. While the lawyers argued, the building sat uncompleted. Some people were convinced it never would be finished.

Finally, new financial backing enabled Frankel to finish and open the hotel in 1975—more than a year late and several million dollars over budget. The 208-room hotel was a showplace. Its highlight: the Club Pompeii, a bar and lounge done up in Roman fashion, complete with toga-clad waitresses, a chariot straight from the movie *Cleopatra* and a twenty-foot-high volcano that "erupted" every hour with a rumbling roar, clouds of smoke and make-believe lava.

But the mountain of debt that went into financing the new hotel topped even the volcano. The steadily worsening financial woes ultimately forced Frankel out, and the hotel shut its doors. It remained closed for more than a year until a group of local businessmen came forward to purchase and reopen it.

In 1982, Harold and Dodi left Huntington and moved to Cape Coral, Florida, where they operated a real estate brokerage firm. He died in Florida in 2002 at age eighty-five.

WOODY WILLIAMS

In the wake of the Japanese attack on Pearl Harbor on December 7, 1941, Hershel Woodrow Williams, a young farm boy from Quiet Dell in Harrison County, West Virginia, tried to enlist in the U.S. Marine Corps. No way, the marines told him. All marine recruits had to be at least five feet, eight inches tall. No matter how straight and tall Williams attempted to stand, he couldn't top five feet, six inches.

But he didn't give up. He just waited. The war continued, and in 1943, the marine corps, badly in need of recruits, did away with its height requirement. Soon Williams—known to family and friends as "Woody"—was on his way to boot camp for basic training. From there, he joined other marines as part of the U.S. island-hopping campaign aimed at rolling back Japan's success in the Pacific.

Williams was sent to New Caledonia, Guadalcanal and Guam. Then, in February 1945, he was part of the huge invasion force that stormed the Japanese stronghold of Iwo Jima. The battle for the island fortress was one of World War II's bloodiest, and it was there that his valor earned Williams the Medal of Honor, the nation's highest military tribute.

The Americans were determined to capture Iwo Jima. Located just 650 miles from Tokyo, it offered a perfect spot to launch bomber attacks on the Japanese homeland. The Japanese were equally determined to hold onto the island and so dug an elaborate system of underground tunnels and man-made hillside caves guarded by machine guns tucked in more than one thousand reinforced concrete pillboxes.

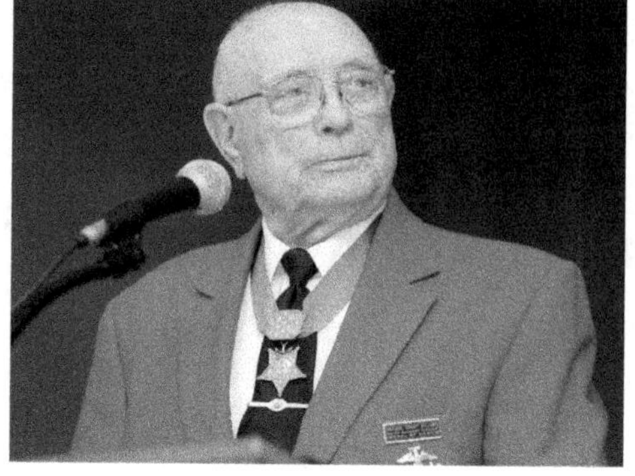

In 1945, when the U.S. Marines stormed Iwo Jima, Woody Williams took out seven Japanese pillboxes—an incredible feat that earned him the Medal of Honor, the nation's highest military decoration. *Herald-Dispatch*.

Bombing and shelling the island for two months did little damage to the entrenched Japanese troops. When the marines charged ashore from their landing craft, their advance was stalled by withering fire from the Japanese. An officer asked for a volunteer to try taking out several pillboxes that had his men penned down.

"I'll see what I can do," Williams said. At least that's what others who were there recall. Williams himself doesn't remember. "Much of this stuff is like a dream," he says. "You wonder if it really happened. And yet some moments are still vivid. It's almost like looking at a slow-motion movie."

Strapping a heavy flamethrower on his back, Williams crawled toward the pillboxes. Once he was close enough, he pulled the trigger, and a ball of flame raced across the ground and into the gun port of the pillbox, incinerating the Japanese inside. Again and again he repeated the process, ignoring the danger involved. Bullets bounced off the tank of jellied gasoline on his back. Any one of them could have exploded the tank, enveloping Williams in flames.

"I remember the Japanese charging out of one of the pillboxes toward me," he says. "I saw bodies, rifles and bayonets. I opened up on 'em. They quit coming."

Williams took out seven pillboxes that day—an incredible feat that soon would have him standing stiffly at attention in the White House Rose Garden as President Truman presented him with the Medal of Honor.

After the war, Williams returned to West Virginia, making his home at Ona in rural Cabell County. He was an official with the Veterans Administration until his retirement, but he never retired from being an advocate for veterans.

"I've thought about Iwo Jima often, but I've thought more about those marines who were killed in that battle and never got to come home," he says. "To me, they are the true heroes."

JOAN C. EDWARDS

Joan Edwards (1918–2006) was born Joan Cavill in London, England, and at the age of four moved with her family to New Orleans, Louisiana. From an early age, she could be heard singing around the house. By the time she was eleven years old, she had already caught the ear of a local manager at WWL Radio who asked her to sing on one of his shows.

When she was thirteen, the radio station had moved to the Roosevelt Hotel, and Edwards, now a veteran performer, was singing with a full orchestra. At seventeen, the fiery, independent Edwards locked horns with her mother regarding her future.

"Mother really wanted me to go to college," she told a magazine interviewer. "But, I wanted to join a girls' orchestra that was going on tour. 'Joan, I don't know if I can allow that,' she told me."

Fortunately for Edwards, a friend of the family was serving as a chaperone for the group, and as was usually the case, Joan got her way. She then set out to see the country. She was with the group for a short time before leaving to sing with Clyde McCoy and his band. While with McCoy, she also made a few movie shorts. From there it was off to Chicago, New York and other cities along the way. By the time she was eighteen, she had already seen much of the country.

Eventually, fate found her in Pittsburgh singing at the William Penn Hotel. In the audience one evening was a young man from Huntington who was working at a division of his father's company—the National Mattress Company. He asked to meet the singer backstage. His name was Jimmy Edwards.

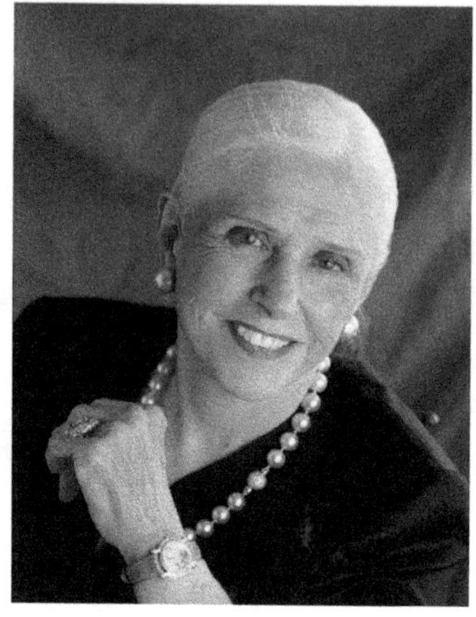

Joan Edwards not only carried out the multimillion-dollar bequests spelled out in her husband's will, she ultimately donated millions more of her own money to Marshall University and other recipients. *Huntington Quarterly*.

The two were soon married at a small ceremony in Pittsburgh. Joan inherited three children from her husband's first marriage. They lived in Pittsburgh for a short time before Jimmy's father summoned the newlyweds to return to Huntington.

Jimmy Edwards had always loved horses. Over the years, that love became a virtual obsession. He progressed from buying racehorses to buying racecourses. At one point, he owned 250 horses and four racetracks.

Jimmy Edwards died in 1991 at age eighty-one. Shortly after his death, his wife of fifty-four years called a press conference and announced that as part of his will, she was presenting $1 million to the Marshall University School of Medicine, $1 million to the Huntington Museum of Art, $2 million to the Episcopal Church, $16 million to Cabell Huntington Hospital for construction of an adult cancer center and contributions to other organizations, including the Cammack Children's Center and the Stella Fuller Settlement.

And that was just the start. Joan Edwards not only carried out the multimillion-dollar bequests spelled out in her late husband's will, she ultimately donated millions more of her own money to Marshall and other recipients.

"Jimmy had family here and he wanted to leave something behind," she explained. "I want to continue what he started."

Ultimately, their contributions totaled more than $65 million.

Marshall has honored her generosity by naming its football stadium, medical school and performing arts center in her honor.

Joan Edwards spent the last few days of her remarkable life receiving treatment and care in the Edwards Comprehensive Cancer Center she helped create at Cabell Huntington Hospital.

PART III

THE STORY CONTINUES

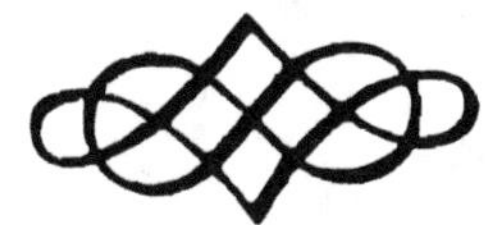

HUNTINGTON HAS HAD THREE CITY HALLS

When Huntington was founded in 1871, its first city hall was a small frame building erected in the 800 block of Fourth Avenue.

In 1886, the city bought a plot of land on the east side of Ninth Street just north of Fifth Avenue and erected Huntington's second city hall—a large red brick structure that housed the city offices, the fire department, the police department and the city jail.

When the county seat was moved from Barboursville to Huntington in 1887, the county government initially shared use of the city building. County officials planned to immediately construct a suitable courthouse and, to that end, purchased the city block bounded by Fourth and Fifth Avenues between Seventh and Eighth Streets. But financial problems delayed a start on construction, with the new courthouse not completed until 1901. It wasn't until then that the county government could be removed from the city building.

In 1911, Huntington's city fathers decided the growing town deserved a larger, grander city hall. They purchased a tract of land on the northeast corner of Fifth Avenue as the site, paying the then-unheard-of sum of $44,000 for it.

Architect Verus T. Ritter was hired to design the new building. One of early Huntington's best-known and most successful architects, Ritter also designed the former Huntington High School building on Eighth Street, the twelve-story Huntington National Bank Building on Fourth Avenue, Johnson Memorial Methodist Church and Central Christian Church.

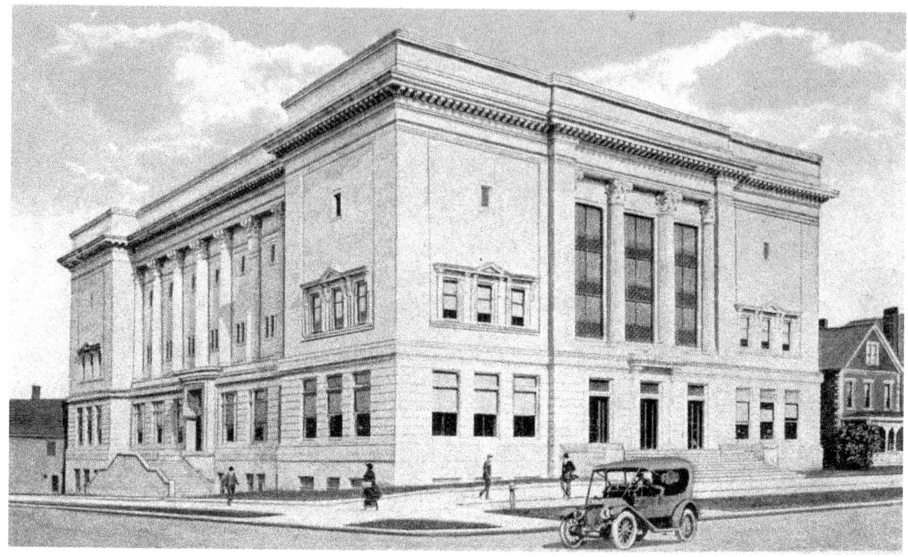

In designing Huntington City Hall, architect Verus T. Ritter combined governmental functions with an ornate 2,500-seat auditorium. Long unused and neglected, the auditorium has since been restored. *Author's collection.*

The King Lumber Company of Charlottesville, Virginia, won the construction contract with a bid of $115,380. Founded in 1899, the firm supplied building materials and skilled workmen for structures in several states. By 1920, it had three hundred employees, making it the largest industrial employer in Charlottesville. It closed in the 1930s, a victim of the Great Depression.

Completed in 1915, the Neoclassic-style building is faced with cream-colored brick with terra-cotta details supplied by the Maryland Terra-cotta Company of Baltimore; limestone quarried in Bedford, Indiana; and granite from Mount Airy, North Carolina.

In designing the new city hall, Ritter combined government functions with an ornate 2,500-seat auditorium. Commenting on the auditorium, City Commissioner John Coon called it "something that the city has needed for a long time."

Once the new city hall was completed and opened, the no-longer-needed city building on Ninth Street was demolished and its site used for construction of a new three-story building for the Deardorff-Sisler department store, which moved there from its former Fourth Avenue location. The department store went out of business in 1930, another victim of the Depression, but its building still stands and now houses offices leased to various tenants.

In the late 1980s, Huntington City Hall was extensively redecorated by the City of Huntington Foundation in a project headed by designer Jean Stephenson. The work included a restoration of the building's auditorium, long abandoned and used only for storage. In 1992, the restored auditorium, again a popular venue for concerts and other events, was named the Jean Stephenson Auditorium in her honor.

CABELL COUNTY COURTHOUSE OPENED ITS DOORS IN 1901

All brides are beautiful, or so it's often said. In the same vein, the word "handsome" is a word regularly employed to describe county courthouses. Seldom has the word been used more aptly than in reference to the Cabell County Courthouse. In his authoritative *Buildings of West Virginia*, noted architectural historian S. Allen Chambers Jr. labels it "perhaps West Virginia's most impressive county courthouse."

A three-story structure of classic Beaux Arts design built of Ohio sandstone, the courthouse stands amid a parklike landscaped setting, with a tall, domed clock tower rising dramatically from the center of its roof. Added to the National Register of Historic Places in 1982, it is the fourth courthouse to serve Cabell County but the only one built in Huntington.

Named for William H. Cabell, who served as Virginia governor from 1805 to 1808, Cabell County was formed in 1809. In creating the new county, Virginia's lawmakers named a commission to locate a county seat, and the commission recommended the courthouse be located in Guyandotte.

In 1813, however, Barboursville was successful in having the county seat moved there, where it remained until the turmoil of the Civil War prompted a temporary move back to Guyandotte. The county seat returned to Barboursville at the war's end and remained there until 1887, when a county referendum approved its move to Huntington.

The move to Huntington was sparked by the new city's rapid growth. Founded by rail tycoon Collis P. Huntington in 1871 as the western terminus of the Chesapeake & Ohio Railway, the town sprang into existence in a very short period of time. In 1880, Huntington's population was fewer than two thousand; by 1890, its population had grown to more than ten thousand. During the 1880s, Huntington gained a water company, paved sidewalks, a telephone system, electric lights, an electric streetcar line and natural gas service.

After its move to Huntington, the county government initially was housed in a building (long since demolished) in the 400 block of Ninth Street that already held Huntington's municipal offices, fire department, police department and jail.

In 1892, the county purchased for $24,757 a courthouse site—a tree-lined square block of land bounded by Fourth and Fifth Avenues and Seventh and Eighth Streets. Plans for construction were delayed by the economic downturn triggered by the Panic of 1893, and it was not until 1895 that the county advertised for plans. The firm of Gunn and Curtis in Kansas City, Missouri, served as architect, and Charles A. Moses of Chicago won the construction contract.

Huntington architect James B. Stewart was hired as supervising architect for the courthouse project. Stewart went on to design a number of the city's finest residences and commercial buildings, including the Carnegie Library, another masterpiece of Beaux Arts design.

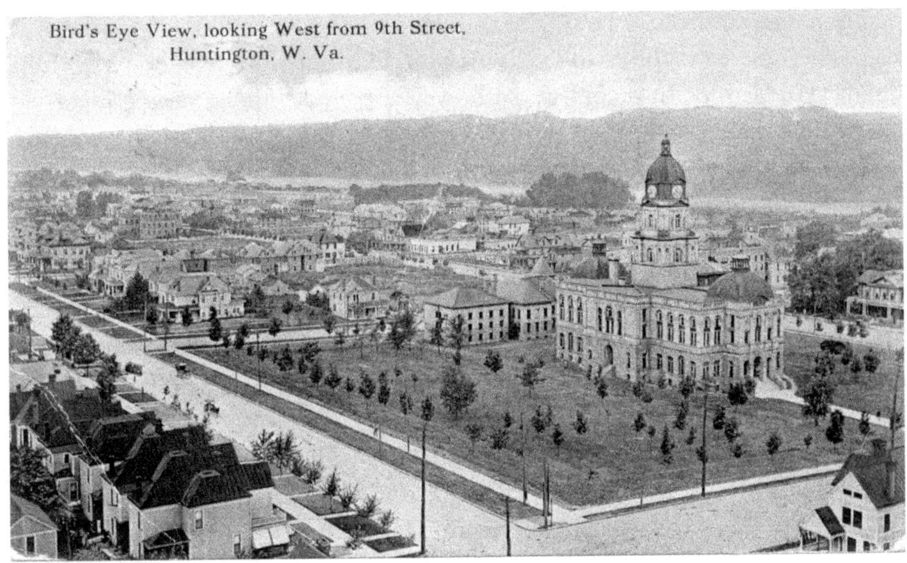

Architectural historian S. Allen Chambers Jr. has proclaimed the Cabell County Courthouse "perhaps West Virginia's most impressive county courthouse." *Author's collection.*

Although the foundation was laid in 1896, more financial woes delayed construction of the superstructure until 1899. The building's cornerstone was laid on November 11, 1899, with—in the words of George S. Wallace, local attorney and historian—"a parade and considerable ceremony." Wallace should know, as he was grand marshal of the parade.

The original building was completed and occupied in December 1901 and then dedicated on February 22, 1902. It cost $95,850 to build, but the county had to sell bonds to finance the project, so that tacked on a nearly equal sum—$83,901—in interest.

Wallace later commented, "After the completion of this new courthouse the people of Cabell County and particularly of the city of Huntington were pleased with, and proud of, the new structure and felt they had provided for the needs of the county for a long time to come."

However, no one anticipated how rapidly Huntington would grow. Before long, the courthouse wasn't large enough to meet the county's needs. So in 1923, a new wing was constructed on the building's west end. Still later, in 1940, a second wing was built on the east end. At the same time, the Depression-era Works Progress Administration funded construction of a new jail on Seventh Street. The west wing cost $133,900 to erect, the east wing cost $208,000 and the new jail cost $246,000.

Over the years, the courthouse was often the victim of slapdash maintenance and outright neglect. In the 1960s, the building's dome was even given a coat of blue and yellow paint, glaringly out of keeping with its Beaux Arts beauty. In recent years, however, county officials and concerned citizens have done much to preserve and restore the old building's grandeur.

The courthouse dome was restored in 1997, with cracks sealed, the mastery refurbished and better lighting installed. Thanks to the generosity of Huntington attorney John Hankins, who dug into his own pocket for the $50,000 it cost, the dome received a coat of genuine gold leaf rather than the gold paint that had been planned. Interior work to the courthouse rotunda—adding new gold and green paint and restoring the ornate decorations on the ceiling—was completed in 2000. And work crews repaired water damage and loose stonework on the building's exterior.

Preserving the historic beauty of the courthouse is important, said Hankins. "Courthouses tend to be the most important building in any county," he said. "We're lucky to have one of the most beautiful in the country."

OLD BANK BUILDING IS HUNTINGTON LANDMARK

Since 1914, when it first opened its doors, the twelve-story building on the southwest corner of Fourth Avenue and Tenth Street has been one of Huntington's best-known structures, a downtown landmark that over the years has attracted business and professional people and their clients, apartment and condominium dwellers and, of course, bank customers.

In 1912, the First National Bank of Huntington acquired the corner lot, demolished the church that stood there and began to construct its grand new building. A decade later, the First National Bank and the Huntington National Bank merged to form the First Huntington National Bank, which would go on to occupy the building for more than fifty years.

Architect Verus T. Ritter designed the bank's new building in the Roman Revival architectural style with Renaissance details.

A Pennsylvania native, the young architect came to Huntington at the urging of his cousin, timber tycoon Charles Lloyd Ritter. Arriving in 1909, he helped design and build C.L. Ritter's twenty-seven-room mansion on Ritter Hill and stayed on to become one of the city's best-known architects of the day. His designs include Johnson Memorial Methodist Church (1913), Huntington City Hall (1915) and Huntington High School (1916). He left Huntington in 1917, moving back to Pennsylvania.

Construction of the bank building was delayed by the 1913 flood, which inundated much of the city's downtown. When the building finally was completed and opened, its office spaces were quickly filled by a variety of businesses, including lawyers, doctors (one of whom even

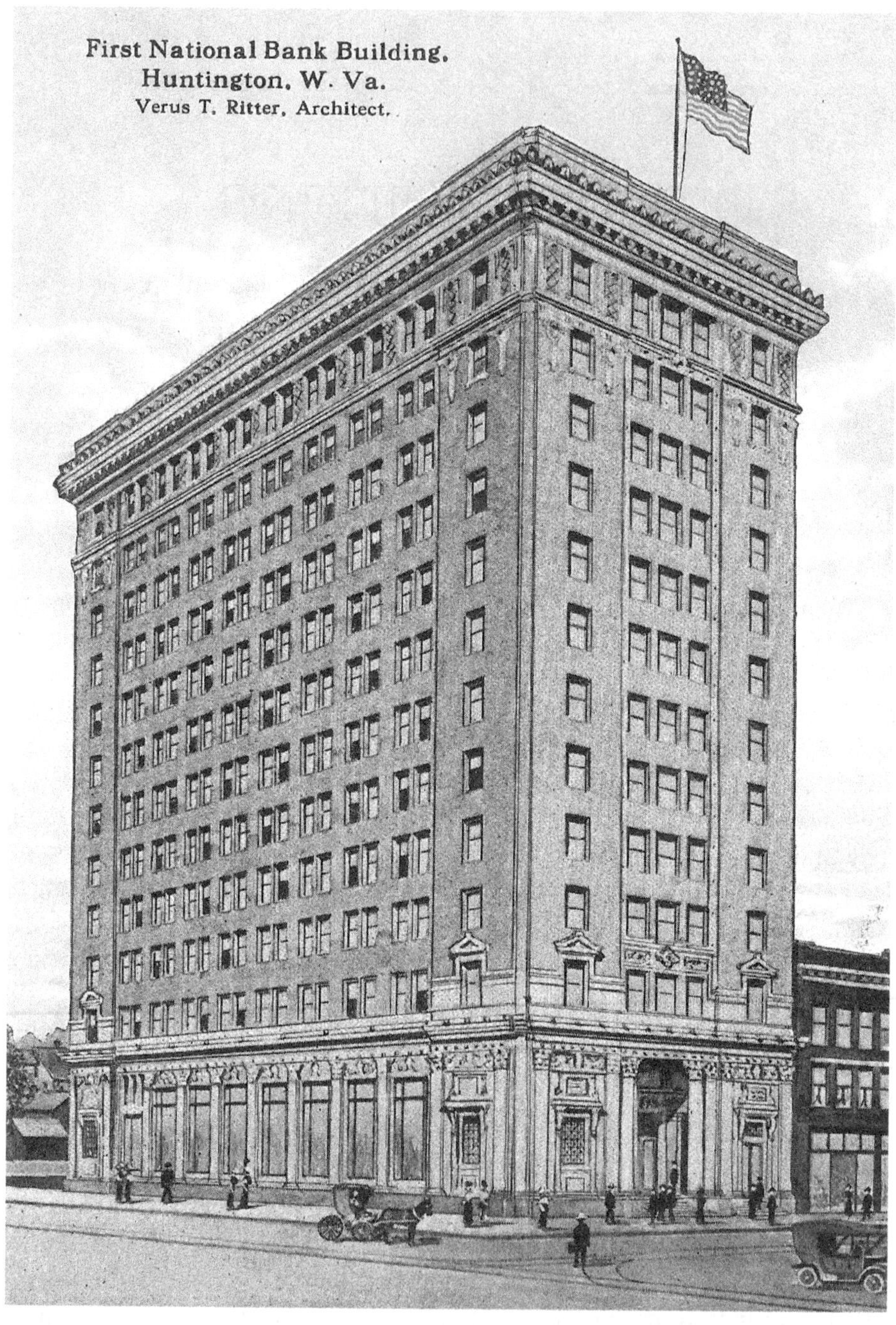

Since it opened in 1914, the bank building on the southwest corner of Fourth Avenue and Tenth Street has been one of downtown Huntington's best-known structures. *Author's collection.*

had a complete operating room), dentists, coal companies, stockbrokers, hairdressers and architects.

The 1925 merger that created the First Huntington National Bank prompted a need for more banking space, so a twelve-story addition was constructed at the rear of the building, extending it to the alley. The architectural firm of Meanor and Handloser copied the original building's design so faithfully that it's difficult to tell where the original structure stops and the addition begins.

The Great Depression hit the country in 1929, causing many banks to fail. The First Huntington National Bank escaped that fate largely due to the ingenuity of its president, Charles M. Gohen. Gohen had the bank's tellers stack piles of currency against the windows of their tell cages, placing a $100 bill on the top of each stack. When many customers entered the bank, ready to withdraw their money, and saw the stacks of currency available, they turned around and left empty-handed. Thus, the bank averted a major crisis—and became the first bank in Huntington to be allowed to resume full operation after the federally mandated "Bank Holiday."

When the Ohio River again flooded the downtown in 1937, the building's basement was flooded, and water seeped into both the main and safety-deposit vaults. While the lobby was spared, all banking services had to be temporarily moved to higher floors. As the floodwaters receded, First Huntington became the first of the city's banks to reopen after the flood.

In 1977, the First Huntington National Bank moved to a new, modern building in the 1000 block of Fifth Avenue as part of Huntington's downtown urban renewal project. In 1981, the newly organized Old National Bank opened in the former First Huntington building on Fourth Avenue.

New owners purchased the Fourth Avenue building in 1987. They invested $6.7 million to buy the building and restore much of its lost luster, renaming it the St. James and revamping its upper floors as offices and luxury residences. Initially, Old National remained as a tenant, but it later closed after its acquisition by City National Bank.

The building became a bank location again with the opening of a Fifth Third Bank branch in 2001. Fifth Third moved out in 2011. The following year, the first State Bank of Barboursville opened a branch in the building, thus becoming the fourth bank to occupy the stately old structure.

VANITY FAIR BUILDING HAS HAD COLORFUL PAST

Huntington's venerable Vanity Fair building has gone through more lives than a cat. Built in 1915, Vanity Fair was, for many years, the only arena in town. Over the decades, it was the scene of countless concerts, carnivals, trade shows, sporting events and other activities.

Heavyweight boxing champ Jack Dempsey fought there, and the annual Golden Gloves amateur boxing tourneys always attracted big crowds. In the 1930s and 1940s, many of the nation's big bands played there. During World War II, young men from throughout the region were bused there for their draft physicals. Until the opening of Veterans Memorial Field House in 1950, it was the home court for Marshall College basketball.

After the war, it hosted a wide range of activities, including country music shows, professional wrestling matches and skating nights. In the 1950s, it became the first studio for Channel 13 television. Today, the old building in the 600 block of Fourth Avenue houses efficiency apartments for low-income residents.

Betty Barrett, founder and president of the Cabell-Huntington Coalition for the Homeless, says she feels certain that if Vanity Fair hadn't been converted to low-income housing, it would have been demolished and the site turned into a parking lot.

A brief article on the front page of the March 13, 1915 issue of the *Advertiser* reported that builder George Watts was ready to begin construction on the new Vanity Fair "exposition hall," a brick and steel structure. "When

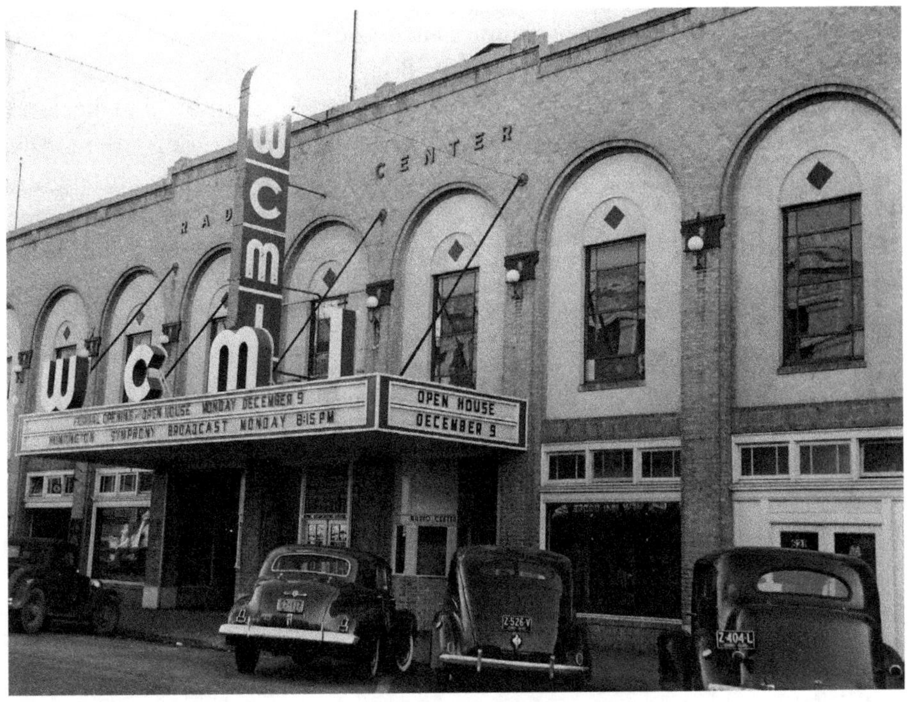

In December 1940, radio station WCMI moved into downtown's Vanity Fair building and gave it a new name: Radio Center. Today, the old building has been converted to apartments for the homeless. *Herald-Dispatch.*

completed," the news story predicted, the new building "will be one of the finest structures of its kind in America."

Beginning in 1916, the building was home to the Fall Festival, an annual trade show sponsored by the Huntington Chamber of Commerce. An early photograph shows the chamber name carved in large letters above the building's main entrance.

The building burned down in 1924 and was rebuilt the following year as the "Vanity Fair Ball Room." An advertisement in the *Herald-Dispatch* on October 4, 1925, billed the new facility as "the Largest and Finest Ball Room in the Ohio Valley" and "a Place of Refinement." A prominent feature of the rebuilding was the installation of a large lighted bandstand at the south end of the arena.

In the late 1920s and early 1930s, dance marathons became a popular fad across America. The marathons were human endurance contests in which couples—generally a mix of local hopefuls and touring professionals—danced almost nonstop for hundreds of hours, competing for prize money. Participants were allowed to rest for fifteen minutes each hour, but they had to spend the rest of the time moving around the dance floor, around the clock.

In 1933, Vanity Fair was the scene of a dance marathon that became the talk of the town. It dragged on for weeks, drawing standing-room-only crowds of spectators. Finally, after an incredible ninety-one days and nights, the contest ended. By that time, of course, the participants were no longer dancing but doing little more than staggering around the floor, doing their best to stay on their feet. With the competition finally over, the winning couple was crowned and each of the two awarded $1,000 in cash—quite a sum in those Depression-era days.

On March 16, 1932, former heavyweight champ Jack Dempsey appeared at Vanity Fair, fighting two exhibition bouts with local boxers. Dempsey stretched one of the two challengers out on the canvas in the first round. The second managed to go the distance but took a real shellacking at Dempsey's hands.

Glenn Miller and his band played there. So did Louis Armstrong, Duke Ellington, Woody Herman and just about every big band great you could think of. Rosemary Clooney sang there. So did Doris Day and the original Ink Spots.

In December 1940, radio station WCMI moved into Vanity Fair and gave it a new name: Radio Center. The station modernized the old place, refinishing the combination dance floor/basketball court and installing permanent stadium-size seats in the balcony, which formerly had been furnished with portable tables and chairs. Outside, the station erected a forty-foot marquee across the front of the building and topped it with a huge neon sign displaying the WCMI call letters.

In 1955, WHTN-TV, Channel 13, went on the air, with its studio located in Radio Center. The station, which later changed its call letters to WOWK, would remain there until 1984, when it moved to a new home at 555 Fifth Avenue. Sharing space in the old building with the TV station was Martin's Restaurant, a popular eatery operated by Johnny Martin.

When WOWK moved out, the building sat vacant for about six years before the Coalition for the Homeless took it over and converted it into fifty-three efficiency apartments. "The fire marshal required us to remove the building's rear wall, where the bandstand was," says Barrett. The result was a big three-sided open-air courtyard with two rows of apartments, the upper units occupying the building's old balcony.

In addition to the apartments, the building is also home to Harmony House, which offers a variety of services to homeless individuals. These include medical/dental care, mental health and substance abuse therapy, employment programs, transportation and such basic needs as laundry, clothing, telephone and mail services.

"Every time I mention Vanity Fair, it triggers memories in people," says Barrett. "I think it's wonderful that a building so many people remember and care about is offering services to people who need help."

RITTER PARK COULD HAVE BEEN SITE OF INCINERATOR

It could have been called Switzer Park. For that matter, but for a fortunate change in plans, it might have been the site of a municipal incinerator. Instead, it became Ritter Park, and it's one of Huntington's best-known and best-loved landmarks. Every day in every season of the year, it attracts countless visitors drawn by its beauty.

It's difficult to imagine there was ever a time when Ritter Park—with its well-tended grassy meadows, its wonderful trees, its handy benches, meandering Four Pole Creek and the bridges that cross it—didn't exist. But believe it or not, there was a time, not so very long ago, when today's expansive park was simply open countryside rarely visited and even less appreciated.

And thereby, as they say, hangs a tale.

The origin of Ritter Park can be traced to the city's earliest years. Oddly enough, Rufus Cook, the Boston surveyor whom rail tycoon Collis P. Huntington hired to lay out his new town, made no provision for a public park. So, as early as 1880, a decade after the city's founding, agitation for a public park began. That year saw the town council vote to issue $7,000 worth of bonds to purchase and designate as parkland three city blocks between Seventh and Eighth Streets north of the Chesapeake & Ohio Railway tracks. But when a referendum election was held, the city's voters turned thumbs-down on the idea.

Later, Huntington himself proposed to sell—not give, mind you, but sell—a tract of land along the C&O tracks east of Fourteenth Street for use

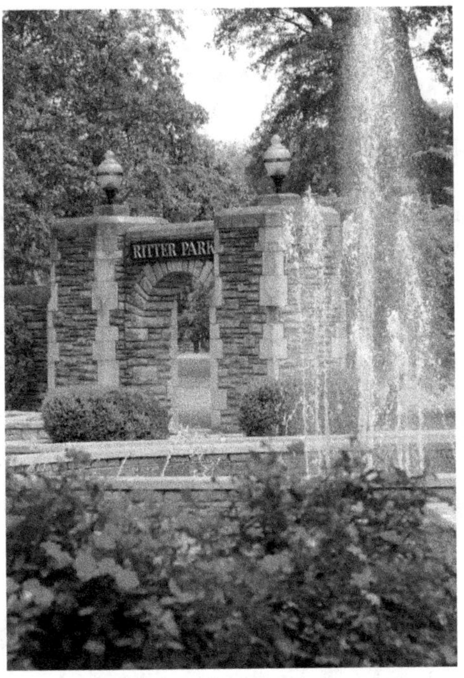

Huntington's seventy-acre Ritter Park has a walking trail, tennis center, children's playground, one-thousand-seat amphitheater, dog park and internationally known Rose Garden. *Huntington Quarterly.*

as a park. But again the voters said no. Various other park ideas were offered over the years, but none proved successful.

Then, in 1908, City Councilman Rufus Switzer was among those involved in the city's purchase of fifty-five acres of land along Four Pole Creek south of Thirteenth Avenue between Eighth and Twelfth Streets. The original plan was to use the land as the site of a city incinerator. But Switzer had a better idea.

At a council meeting, Switzer proposed that the land instead be used as the city's first public park. Hard as it might be to believe today, Switzer's proposal encountered strong opposition, with critics charging that the tract was too far outside the city. (At that time, most of the city lay between the Ohio River on the north and the C&O tracks on the south.)

Once he became mayor, Switzer continued to fight hard for his idea. Along the way, he gained an important ally, businessman Charles Lloyd Ritter, who didn't welcome the idea of an incinerator just downhill from his estate on Eighth Street Hill. Ritter offered to donate additional acreage to the city if all the land was designated as a park. The city not only took him up on his offer but also proceeded to name the park in his honor.

Reelected as mayor, Switzer recruited a well-known New Jersey landscape architect, J.T. Withers, to draw up a master plan for the new park. But before work could get started, Switzer was defeated in a bid for a third term as mayor. The new administration abandoned the park plan, and the property went largely unused.

The development of today's Ritter Park largely dates from the establishment of the Huntington Board of Park Commissioners in 1925. With local attorney George S. Wallace at the helm, the board set about creating a park the city could be proud of. Special attention was lavished on the nationally known Rose Garden. Tennis players flocked to the park's courts, while oldsters enjoyed a seemingly endless game of croquet on the park's broad meadow.

During the Great Depression of the 1930s, the federal Works Progress Administration employed talented stonemasons who constructed handsome walls and walkways that still beautify the park.

But the grand old park was showing its age by the 1980s, when a new director, James McClelland, took charge and introduced a number of welcome innovations. The park's amphitheater was refurbished, a new picnic shelter was constructed and a "tennis bubble" was installed that permits year-round play.

A new building was constructed at the Rose Garden. Starkly modern in its design and named "The Room with a View," the structure provides an indoor setting for weddings and other events.

And in what proved to be a hugely popular addition to the park, a mile-long, oval-shaped walking and jogging track was constructed. The track attracts determined users in all but the worst of weather, and a sunny afternoon or balmy evening will see it filled with people of all ages. Nodding and saying, "Hi there!" to friends and neighbors encountered on the pathway is now a familiar ritual for many.

In recent years, the children's playground was expanded and updated and a graceful fountain constructed at the park's Tenth Street entrance. In 2012, a fenced dog park opened. National attention was focused on Ritter Park that year, when the American Planning Association (APA) named it as one of the "10 Great Public Places in America."

"Ritter Park demonstrates how a public space, through its design and attractions, can serve diverse interests and provide a range of experiences," said APA chief Paul Farmer. "It also illustrates how a well-planned park can influence and add values to the homes and properties that surround it."

SIXTH STREET BRIDGE OPENED IN 1926

Legend has it that one evening in the 1920s, millionaire Huntington businessman Charles Lloyd Ritter threw a history-making dinner party. Ritter invited the elite of the city's business leadership to his imposing mansion on Eighth Street Hill, where he wined and dined them and then sprang a surprise. As the evening drew to a close, he informed his guests that nobody would be allowed to leave until they got out their checkbook and wrote a check to his newly formed Huntington-Ohio Bridge Company.

Maybe that's the way it happened, and maybe not. A good story is sometimes just that—a story.

But whatever methods Ritter may have employed, it's an unassailable fact that by early 1925, he had enlisted more than a dozen of the city's best-known business leaders in his bold plan to build a bridge across the Ohio River linking Huntington and the Ohio village of Chesapeake.

The need for a bridge across the Ohio was obvious. In 1869, when town founder Collis P. Huntington entrusted his brother-in-law Delos W. Emmons with the task of purchasing land for the new town that Huntington envisioned, he reminded Emmons to make certain to buy a tract of Ohio land that would be suitable for that end of a bridge—a span the canny railroad mogul knew the community would need. And yet, in the 1920s, more than a half century later, there was still no bridge. The only way of crossing the Ohio at Huntington was by ferryboat.

Ritter and other Huntington business leaders were convinced that if the city was to continue to grow and prosper, a bridge across the Ohio was essential. So they set about building one.

A site at Sixth Street, just west of the city's downtown business district, was chosen, and construction began in April 1925. An estimated ten thousand spectators turned out for the dedication ceremony on May 23, 1926, when the first cars and trucks rolled across the new span.

As completed, the two-lane bridge and its approaches stretched for a combined length of a bit more than half a mile. The roadway was twenty-two feet in width with a broad sidewalk to accommodate pedestrians. A tollbooth was tucked onto the side of the bridge.

The basic toll to cross the bridge was twenty-five cents for cars, with an additional five cents for each passenger. The toll for pedestrians and bicyclists was five cents. Truck tolls ranged as high as one dollar, depending on the weight of the truck. You could ride your motorcycle across for ten cents, but if it had a sidecar, you had to pay fifteen cents.

People flocked to use the long-needed bridge, which did a brisk business even in the Depression years, when quarters to pay the toll were hard to come by for many motorists.

The bridge remained in private hands until 1940, when its owners sold it to Cabell County for $2 million. In 1952, county officials, worried about their ability to finance needed maintenance and repairs for the span, turned it over to the State of West Virginia.

More and more traffic crossed the bridge each year. Evening rush hours saw traffic in downtown Huntington snarled for blocks as motorists lined up and waited their turn to cross the span. Mornings brought a similar traffic snarl in Chesapeake. As early as the 1950s, traffic studies indicated a need for an additional bridge or bridges.

On December 15, 1967, the Silver Bridge at Point Pleasant, West Virginia, collapsed into the Ohio, killing forty-five people. That disaster fed a growing public distrust of the rickety Sixth Street Bridge—and prompted increasingly louder demands for a new bridge.

But it wasn't until 1968 that Huntington got a second Ohio River bridge—a two-lane toll bridge built at West Seventeenth Street and later named for Representative Nick J. Rahall (D-WV).

The tolls had been removed from the Sixth Street Bridge when the state took it over in 1952 but were restored in 1969 to help pay for construction of the new bridge at West Seventeenth Street. The tolls were finally lifted at both spans in 1978.

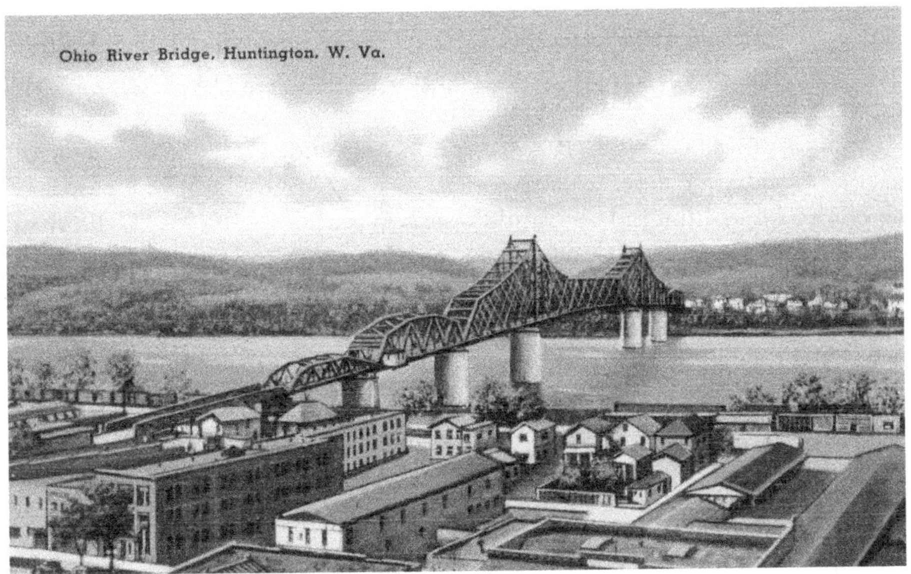

In 1926, businessman C.L. Ritter and his partners built Huntington's first Ohio River bridge at Sixth Street, just west of the city's downtown. Long outmoded, the decrepit span was demolished in 1995. *Author's collection.*

Originally, plans called for construction of a third bridge in Huntington immediately after the West Seventeenth Street Bridge was built, but funding problems and controversy over selecting a site delayed its construction for decades. When the East Huntington Bridge was finally built in 1985, the towering suspension span proved to be a thing of beauty. The third bridge ultimately was named for Marshall University football great Frank "Gunner" Gatski. But, like its predecessors, it was only two lanes.

Huntington wouldn't get a four-lane Ohio River bridge until 1994.

State highway officials initially favored "rehabilitating" the long-obsolete Sixth Street Bridge, but a close inspection showed that the rusted relic was beyond saving. So the state set about building a new bridge that, when it opened, was named for West Virginia's legendary Senator Robert C. Byrd.

Work on the new bridge at a site adjacent to the Sixth Street Bridge forced the closure of the old bridge in the summer of 1993, bringing an end to its many decades of service to the motoring public.

Once the Byrd Bridge was open, the state readied plans to demolish the Sixth Street Bridge. Some in Huntington protested, arguing that the bridge should be preserved and turned into a pedestrian span with small shops and eating places. But nobody seemed to know how to go about making that happen—or how to come up with the millions of dollars the project would surely require. So the idea died at birth.

And so on February 2, 1995, a loud bang ended sixty-eight years of history. Carefully placed explosive charges rocked the Sixth Street Bridge, severing its four-hundred-foot middle section and dropping it into the river below. Later, the bridge's two towers were dropped into the Ohio and the tangled scrap metal pulled from the water to be sent off for recycling.

In the spring of 1995, the bridge's concrete piers were blasted out of the river. And the old Sixth Street Bridge passed into Huntington history.

FLOODWALL HAS PROTECTED CITY FOR SEVENTY-PLUS YEARS

When rail tycoon Collis P. Huntington picked the site for the town that today carries his name, he was looking for a good spot to transfer passengers and cargo between the trains of the Chesapeake & Ohio Railway and the Ohio River's steamboats.

Huntington chose well, and his new town thrived. But like other Ohio River communities, the young Huntington was regularly visited by damaging floods. Every few years, the Ohio would surge out of its banks and inundate the growing town. When the water receded, folks would roll up their sleeves, clean up the mess and get back to work. But nobody living in Huntington or elsewhere in the Ohio Valley was prepared for what happened in 1937.

January of that year was unusually warm. Winter's rapidly melting snow cover combined with nineteen straight days of heavy rain to create just the right conditions for flooding along the Ohio's entire 981-mile length from Pittsburgh to Cairo, Illinois, where it joins the Mississippi.

The resulting flood, the Ohio's worst ever, inundated thousands of homes, businesses, factories and farms in a half dozen states; drove a million people from their homes; claimed nearly four hundred lives; and recorded $500 million in damages. Taking inflation into account, that figure would translate into more than $7 billion today.

At 11:00 a.m. on January 27, 1937, the Ohio reached a depth of 69.45 feet at Huntington. That was more than 19.00 feet above the official flood stage and 3.00 feet higher than the previous record high, set in 1913. The raging water flooded most of the city's downtown and drove thousands of residents from their homes. People in rowboats made their way along downtown's Fourth Avenue. Relief centers, set up in undamaged churches and schools, struggled to feed as many as nine thousand people a day. When the river receded, five people were dead and the city was a soggy ruin.

Could a new flood as damaging as 1937's strike the Ohio Valley again? Experts say that's unlikely but not impossible. If that happened, however, Huntington would be safe and dry behind the massive floodwall that has protected it for nearly seventy years.

The Huntington District U.S. Army Corps of Engineers, which built the floodwall in the wake of the '37 flood, estimates that since its completion in 1943, the wall has prevented $250 million in flood damages to Huntington homes and businesses. Figure in the inflation factor and that would be $2 billion in today's dollars.

But what if the floodwall had never been built?

History shows that in fact might have been the case except for the efforts of the Huntington Chamber of Commerce and its president, Colonel Joseph H. Long. The chamber waged a determined fight to get the wall built, an effort that even included a legal challenge that went all the way to the West Virginia Supreme Court.

Dr. W.S. Rosenheim, the chamber's managing director, and Long, publisher of the *Advertiser* and chairman of the chamber, worked tirelessly to see the floodwall built. On February 18, 1937, even as the waters of that year's record-setting flood were still receding, Long appointed a chamber committee to study construction of a floodwall.

The following June 15, the two men, along with City Engineer John S. Gillespie, traveled to Washington, D.C., to urge congressional action on flood protection for Huntington and other communities along the Ohio.

Testifying before the House Committee on Flood Control, Chief of Engineers Edward Markham used photographs of the flood at Huntington to illustrate the need for flood protection. He told the committee that Huntington had been flooded twenty-three times in fifty-five years and that the 1937 flood had inundated the business section to an average depth of eleven feet and caused losses estimated at more than $14 million.

In *Men, Mountains and Rivers*, his history of the Huntington District Corps of Engineers, river historian Leland R. Johnson quotes Markham as saying that while flood control projects obviously could be justified by the monetary loss they would prevent, it was his opinion that the real justification lay in "the saving of human life and suffering, and in the prevention of the disturbance of the affairs of the nation brought about by a flood disaster."

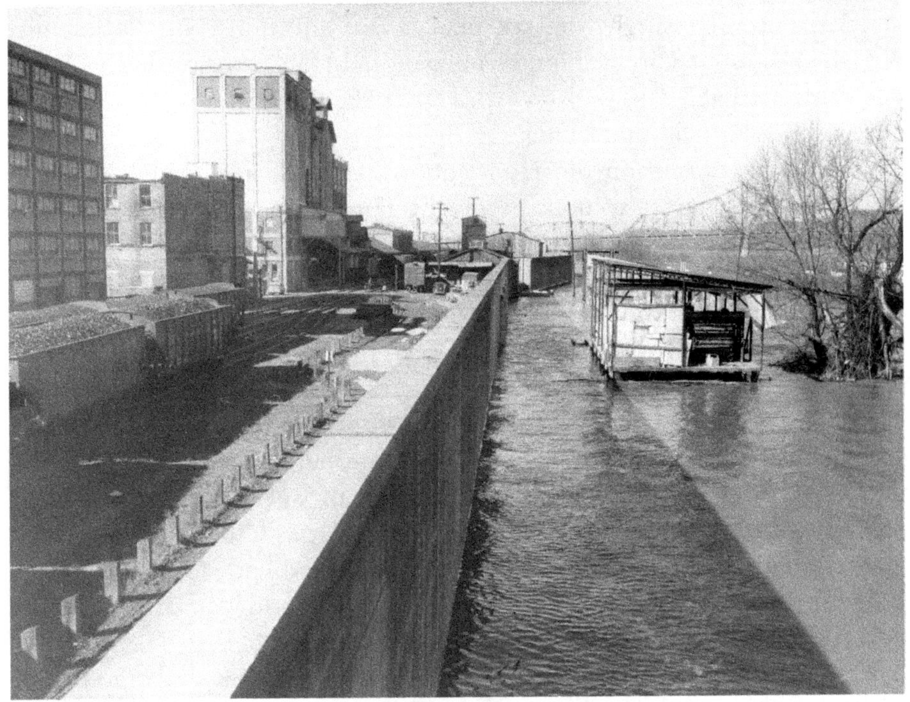

Even before the record-setting 1937 Ohio River flood had receded, efforts were started to build a protective floodwall for Huntington. The wall was completed in 1943. *Herald-Dispatch.*

Representative George W. Johnson (D-WV) told the committee that Huntington was "eternally and everlastingly, every year" suffering flood damages far above the costs of local cooperation and was ready and willing to contribute its share.

Rosenheim told the committee that Huntington, "if necessary," would accept the responsibility of providing rights-of-way for a floodwall. "Huntington was hit awfully hard" in that year's flood, he said. "But we need flood protection so badly that if it is impossible for the federal government to provide full payment, the city will undertake to provide the property."

Congress ultimately approved a plan along those lines. Accordingly, the chamber set about identifying the rights-of-way needed for the Huntington wall—and figuring out how to pay for securing them.

Huntington City Council voted to sell bonds to finance the land acquisition and then repay the bond money with the proceeds of a new "floodwall tax" that would be levied on all property the wall would protect.

Perhaps not surprisingly, the tax plan drew objections—and a lawsuit. A Cabell County Circuit Court ruling upheld the legality of the bond sale and floodwall tax, and on April 9, 1938, the State Supreme Court unanimously upheld that ruling.

Once work started on the Huntington floodwall, it was built in three sections, with separate sections protecting Huntington, Westmoreland and Guyandotte. Construction of the wall's Huntington section began on August 1, 1938, and was completed in 1940, with work crews then moving to the Westmoreland section.

The outbreak of World War II prompted the corps to halt all civil works projects so that material and workers could be shifted to military projects. The sole exception to that halt was the Guyandotte floodwall, deemed essential to protecting the plant of the International Nickel Company (INCO). The plant was then busily engaged in war work, including the production of materials vital to the Manhattan Project, the top-secret effort that was building the atomic bomb. The 1937 flood had closed the INCO plant for six weeks. A similar shutdown during World War II could have meant a real setback for the war effort.

The Huntington Floodwall Board took over the operation and maintenance of the completed floodwall in 1943. Early in that year, the floodwall prevented about $3.0 million in damages, and in March 1945, the wall saved the city another $3.6 million in damages.

On completion of the floodwall, a bronze plaque was placed at its Tenth Street gate honoring "the public-spirited citizens whose vision and foresight" made possible the wall's construction. The wall, the plaque reads, "was initiated by the Chamber of Commerce" and "designed and constructed under the supervision of the United States Army Engineers."

Construction of the floodwall brought one negative side effect. With the wall blocking the Ohio from daily view, the city essentially turned its back on the river and forgot it was there. Fortunately, the construction of Harris Park changed that. Dedicated in 1984, the riverfront park represented a welcome rediscovery of the river by the community it helped create.

STATE HOSPITAL BLAZE CLAIMED SEVENTEEN VICTIMS

It was Thanksgiving Eve 1952. Most of the community was in a festive mood, already relaxing and looking forward to the next day's holiday.

Then, shortly after 7:00 p.m., the bells started ringing at the Huntington Fire Department's old Alarm Headquarters on Ninth Street. The automated alarm system indicated a fire at the Huntington State Hospital on Norway Avenue. No one knew it in those first hectic minutes, but the alarm triggered what would be one of the most horrific chapters in the city's history.

The death toll in the 1952 fire at the State Hospital remains Huntington's worst ever. Fourteen women and girls died that night. Doctors at the scene said one victim burned to death and ten others suffocated from smoke. Three more victims died of their injuries in the following days. The oldest victim was eighty-nine. The youngest was eleven.

Sirens screaming, firefighters raced to the scene. There, they found an old brick ward building in flames. A fire had erupted in the basement boiler room and quickly spread to the first floor. Women and children housed in the three-story structure frantically screamed for help as firefighters used hammers, chisels and anything else they could find to batter away at the building's heavy wire-mesh window screens. Ultimately, they had to cut through the mesh with acetylene torches to gain entry to the building.

The flames were confined to the building's first two floors, but thick, acrid smoke blanketed everything, hampering the firefighters' efforts. It took two hours to bring the fire under control, and for much of that time, the smoke

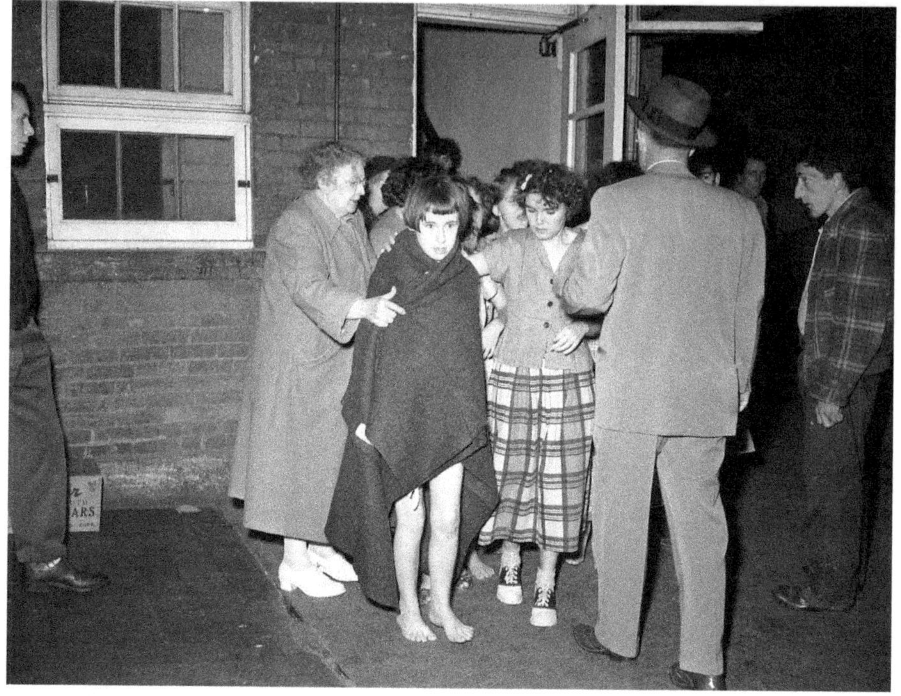

The deadly 1952 fire at the Huntington State Hospital came at a time of growing public concern about conditions at the antiquated, overcrowded hospital. The Thanksgiving Eve fire claimed the lives of seventeen patients. *Herald-Dispatch.*

trapped the young patients who were housed on the building's third floor. Fire Captain Harry Damron supervised the evacuation of thirty-five to forty children from the third floor of the burning structure

Gene Wheeler, a twenty-eight-year-old firefighter at the time, later recalled making his way into the burning building and finding a young girl, maybe seven years old, tied to her bed, unable to move. Wheeler managed to untie and rescue her. Wheeler also remembered seeing fellow firefighter John Cannon carry a teenage girl to safety. (Twenty years later, in 1972, Cannon suffered a fatal heart attack while fighting a spectacular fire at the former Standard Ultramarine & Color Company plant.)

Damron said that after it was thought all the patients had been evacuated to safety, he found a woman wrapped in a blanket and lying on the floor under a bed. She was suffering from shock, he said.

The building housed 275 women and children that terror-filled night. Aided by members of the hospital's staff and some of the male patients, firefighters managed to rescue most of them.

The screaming patients had to be removed by means of an old wrought-iron circular stairway at the rear of the building. Rescuers couldn't use stretchers on the narrow stairway, so they bundled the patients—some alive, some dead—in blankets and carried them down on their shoulders. Once the mesh screens were removed from the windows, some patients were carried down ladders positioned at the windows.

The ward building had been designed to lock patients in, with apparently little thought given as to how they might get out in case of a fire or other emergency.

Meals for the patients were prepared in a kitchen located in another building on the hospital campus. As victims were carried out of the burning ward building, the kitchen was turned into a makeshift receiving station for them.

A reporter on the scene that night described it as a "sorry sight."

"The patients," the reporter wrote, "were sprawled on the kitchen floor, some of them dead, most with only a blanket covering them, reeking with the strong smell of smoke."

The *Herald-Dispatch* quoted Police Captain Hercil H. Gartin as saying that a score of the city's doctors and as many nurses responded to a police appeal for medical help at the scene.

Fire Chief Floyd E. Crouse said all Huntington firefighters who were on duty were deployed at the hospital, along with fifteen others who were off duty but were called in to help fight the fire and evacuate patients.

A number of volunteers aided the firefighters in the evacuation. Dr. Hiram Davis, the hospital's superintendent, praised their efforts. "I cannot be too generous in my praise of the work of the firemen and volunteers," Davis said. "I saw boys of high school age helping carry litters. No one had asked them. They just volunteered. The firemen were very efficient. We owe much to them."

No official ruling was made as to the fire's cause, although speculation suggested it was started by a carelessly discarded cigarette. Smoking was officially banned in the building, but smokers—patients and staff members alike—frequently ignored the ban, going to the basement to light up.

The fire came at a time of growing public concern about conditions at the old hospital, established as an insane asylum in 1897 and originally called the Home for Incurables. In 1901, the name was changed to West Virginia Asylum, and in 1916, the name was changed again, this time to Huntington State Hospital. Although the name was changed, the institution's operating philosophy remained much the same as when it first opened—to protect society from the mentally ill by locking them away in a place where they received little, if any, treatment.

By the time of the fire, a hospital designed to accommodate 500 patients was home to nearly 1,800. Medical staffing was grossly inadequate, with only a handful of trained doctors and nurses and attendants who were few in number, virtually untrained and poorly paid. The hospital's buildings were antiquated and poorly maintained.

Ironically, a new building was under construction on the night of the fatal fire, and a hospital official told reporters the patients in the building that burned were scheduled to be transferred to the new building within a few weeks.

But despite new construction and other sporadic improvements, conditions at the hospital remained a subject of concern until the 1970s, when the patient population began to decline as a result of deinstitutionalization. In 1988, Huntington State became the first state-operated psychiatric hospital in West Virginia to be accredited by the Joint Commission on Accreditation of Healthcare Organizations.

In 1995, the West Virginia legislature changed the facility's name to Huntington Hospital. And in 1999, Governor Cecil Underwood announced its renaming as the Mildred Mitchell-Bateman Hospital, a tribute to her lifetime career of helping the mentally ill. Today, the hospital is a 110-bed acute care mental health facility.

FORMER GARBAGE DUMP WAS SACRED GROUND TO GRID FANS

For more than sixty years, a former garbage dump on Huntington's South Side was sacred ground for Thundering Herd football fans. From 1928 to 1990, Fairfield Stadium was the home of the Herd. The old red brick stadium was also the site of countless high school football games and a wide variety of other events.

The history of Fairfield Stadium can be traced back to the West Virginia legislature's 1925 creation of the Huntington Board of Park Commissioners. One provision of the park board's charter empowered it to join with what was then Marshall College and/or the Cabell County Board of Education in constructing a stadium.

Perhaps not surprisingly, there was immediate disagreement about a suitable site. Marshall wanted to locate the stadium either on campus or adjacent to it. The Huntington Chamber of Commerce argued that League Park in West Huntington would be a better choice. But from the first, the park board had its eye on a piece of South Side property about a half dozen blocks from the Marshall campus—a tract of land bordered by Charleston and Columbia Avenues between Fourteenth and Fifteenth Streets.

Originally a gravel pit owned and operated by Huntington businessman W.M. Prindle, the property had been briefly leased by the city and used as a garbage dump. Eventually, the park board's choice prevailed, and it paid Prindle $25,000 to purchase the property.

More disagreements followed about how best to go about constructing and operating the stadium, but finally the park board, Marshall and the school

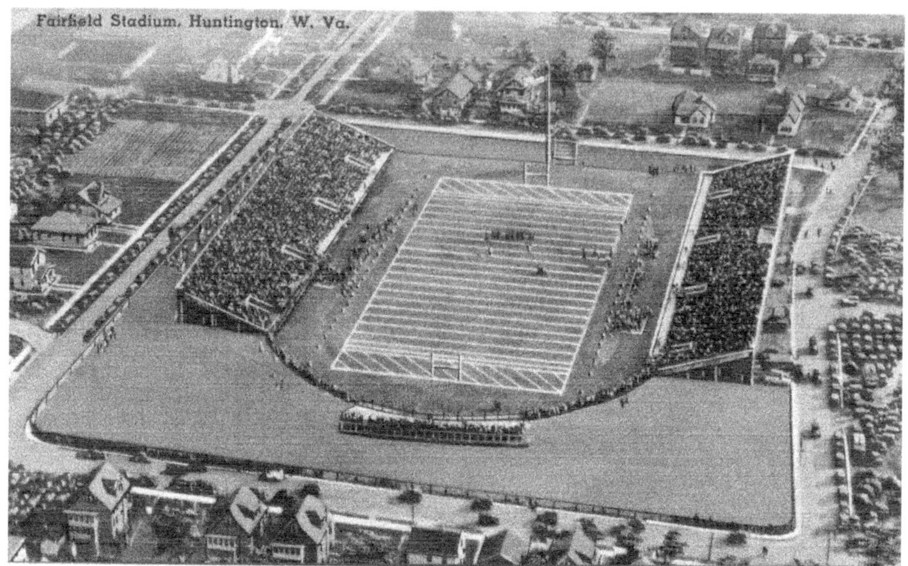

For more than sixty years, venerable Fairfield Stadium was the home of Marshall football, along with high school grid games and a variety of other events. *Author's collection.*

board ironed out a three-way agreement, and construction of the stadium began. The Huntington architectural firm of Meanor and Handloser was hired for the project.

When discussion turned to selecting a name for the stadium, George S. Wallace, the park board's longtime president, jokingly proposed "Cockroach Commons," a reference to the property's former use as a garbage dump. On a more serious note, former property owner Prindle suggested that the stadium be named Fairfield after his home county of Fairfield in Ohio, and his idea prevailed.

What was finally called Fairfield Municipal Stadium saw its first football game on September 29, 1928, when Huntington High defeated Portsmouth (Ohio) High, 18–0. The first touchdown scored in the new stadium was by Bobby McComas, Ramey Hunter had the honor of the initial kickoff and Red Jackson made the first tackle—all for Huntington High. The crowd was estimated at 6,500.

Marshall didn't play its first game at Fairfield until the following October 6, when it teamed up with Huntington High for a doubleheader and the stadium's official dedication ceremonies. In the day's first game, HHS defeated Logan High, 21–0, and then Marshall made it a double whitewash by routing Fairmont State College, 27–0.

According to notes in the Dedication Day Program, the completed stadium had eleven thousand seats, a mechanical scoreboard donated by the Huntington Publishing Company and "an extraordinary public address system." The program said the stadium's cost was "approximately $200,000."

Over the years, Fairfield would be home field for football teams from Huntington High, Huntington East High and Douglass High, the county's pre-integration black school. In addition to football, Fairfield played host to a variety of events over the course of its history.

For many years, bands from throughout the state descended on Huntington every May for the West Virginia High School Band Festival. Organized for the first time in 1935, the festival not only included a big parade through town but also precision marching and maneuvers at Fairfield. During its heyday in the early 1950s, the festival attracted dozens of bands and thousands of young musicians, their bright uniforms turning the stadium into a kaleidoscope of color. By 1967, the festival had grown too large for one city to handle and was divided into regional competitions. The stadium maneuvers were discontinued.

In 1959, Cabell County celebrated its 150th anniversary with a mammoth outdoor pageant at Fairfield called "Cabellrama," which featured 1,500 actors, actresses, singers and dancers. In 1964, when famed evangelist Billy Graham came to Huntington, Fairfield was the only place in town large enough to accommodate the huge crowd.

From the outset, Fairfield's three-way ownership never worked well. With nobody solely in charge, maintenance was neglected, and the once-proud stadium was allowed to deteriorate. In 1962, the situation became so dire that the city building inspector slapped a CONDEMNED sign on the stadium, declaring it unsafe for public use. Modest repairs were made to keep the stadium open, but it was clear that more had to be done.

Marshall voiced a willingness to dramatically upgrade Fairfield but only if it became the stadium's sole owner. In 1970, the park board and the school board gladly gave up their shared ownership. Marshall then installed an Astroturf playing surface, built new dressing rooms and made room for 6,800 more seats by lowering the field.

But even with those improvements, it was clear that Fairfield was living on borrowed time. In 1984, an inspection showed that the stadium's east-side stands were in danger of collapsing, so the upper level of the stands was demolished and replaced with new bleacher-type seating.

Finally, with construction well underway on what would become Marshall's $30 million Joan C. Edwards Stadium, Marshall played its last football game at Fairfield on November 10, 1990, losing to Eastern Kentucky University, 15–12.

In departing Fairfield, the Herd left behind one of the poorest excuses for a stadium found anywhere in college football, but the school also left behind some splendid memories.

Surely none of the memories of old Fairfield burns brighter than Marshall's September 25, 1971 stunning victory over Xavier. In the wake of the November 14, 1970 jetliner crash that claimed the lives of seventy-five Marshall players, coaches and fans, many urged that the school abandon football. Instead, Marshall patched together a team that sportswriters and fans christened the "Young Thundering Herd." The Xavier game was the second of the 1971 season and Marshall's home opener.

Marshall took the field a three-touchdown underdog. But with one second in the game, quarterback Reggie Oliver hit tailback Jerry Gardner on a bootleg pass, and Gardner scampered thirteen yards for the winning touchdown as the Young Herd defeated Xavier, 15–3.

As proud Herd coach Jack Lengyel proclaimed after the game, "No one thought we had a chance to win except the team." An hour and a half after game's end, the Fairfield stands were still full as the crowd continued celebrating.

After Marshall left for its new stadium, Fairfield stood mostly unused. The dressing rooms were remodeled to house Marshall's Forensic Science Center, and nearby Cabell Huntington Hospital began using the playing field for an overflow parking lot. Then came the decision to use the Fairfield site for construction of the medical school's $23.5 million Erma Ora Byrd Clinical Center, and so the wrecking crews began work on what was left of the venerable old stadium.

Today, Fairfield is gone, but the cherished memories—like 1971's "miracle" victory over Xavier—remain. Listen closely and you can still hear the cheers.

FIELD HOUSE SERVED THE COMMUNITY WELL

Veterans Memorial Field House served the Huntington community well for more than sixty years—while struggling with one fiscal crisis after another.

The genesis of the Field House can be traced to 1945, when the West Virginia legislature established the Cabell County Recreation Board. Initially, the board was charged with supervising a network of twenty playgrounds scattered through the county. But Chairman Max Jones and his fellow board members had far bigger things in mind.

At the time, Huntington's only public arena was Radio Center, located in the 600 block of Fourth Avenue. Originally named Vanity Fair when it was built in 1915, the old building had been modernized a bit but was still no longer up to being the home court for Marshall College basketball or the many other events conducted there.

Jones was manager of the old Huntington Water Corporation (now part of West Virginia American Water) and one of the community's best-known civic leaders. He and others in the community were convinced that an up-and-coming town like Huntington needed a modern arena and set about laying the groundwork for its construction.

In 1948, the Cabell County Court (now Commission) gave the recreation board $75,000 to hire an architect and do other preliminary work on a new arena. The following year, the county issued $830,000 in bonds to finance its construction.

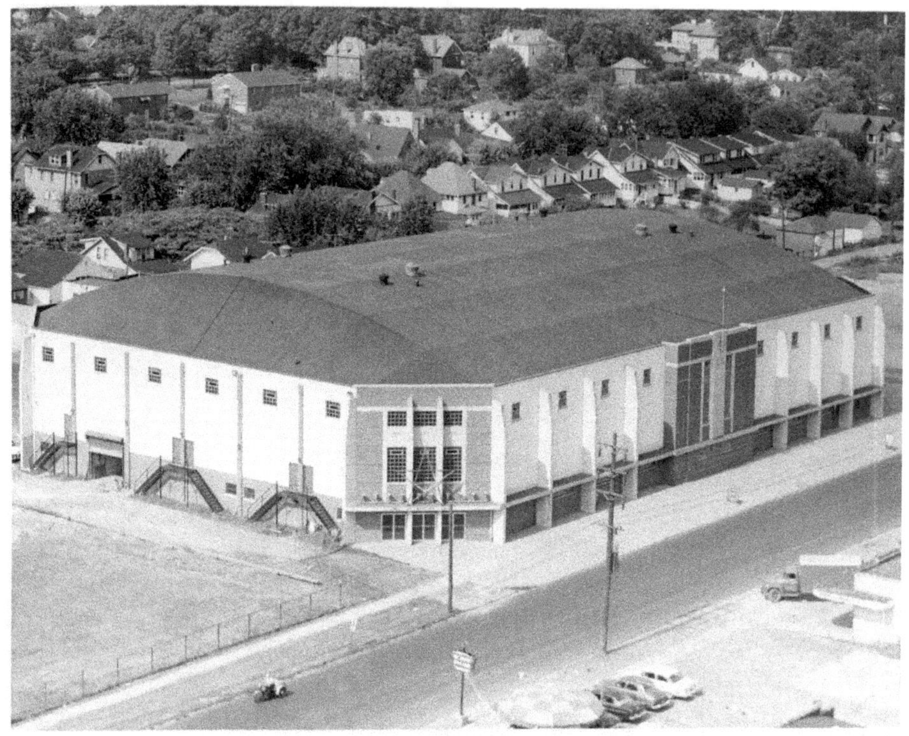

Veterans Memorial Field House officially opened with a choral pageant by school youngsters, but for basketball fans, the real opening came a few days later when Marshall played its first game there. *Author's collection.*

Construction of what would become Veterans Memorial Field House began in August 1949 with Lewis Stettler as architect, C.H. Jimison & Sons of Huntington as the general contractor and a laundry list of other local companies as subcontractors. A forty-five-day industry-wide strike that year sent steel prices up, and the project's backers soon found they didn't have enough money to complete and equip the building. So they went back to the county and asked for additional funding. The result was a second bond issue, one for $175,000. Both bond issues were to be paid back over a twenty-nine-year span with an annual interest rate of 3.75 percent. The two bond issues were to spell big trouble for the arena once it was completed and opened.

The new structure was officially named Veterans Memorial Field House, and a dedicatory panel was placed on the Fifth Avenue side of the building reading: "Erected 1950 A.D. Dedicated to Those Who Gave in Freedom's Cause the Last Full Measure of Devotion—1917–1918, 1941–1945."

The first event at the new Field House came on November 13, 1950, when "Holiday on Ice" began a four-day engagement. The ice show provided the crowd of five thousand their first chance to experience the new arena. Most people seemed to like what they saw. In his review of the show, *Advertiser* reporter John McClane enthusiastically praised it but noted that the Field House "all but stole the show before the program began."

The second show to play the Field House came roughly two weeks later, on November 29—featuring singing cowboy star Roy Rogers; his wife, Dale Evans; and, of course, his horse Trigger.

The building's official opening was November 30 with a choral pageant featuring 2,430 students from the county's schools. But for many fans, the real opening event came on December 2, when the Marshall men's basketball team played the first of its more than four hundred games at the Field House—an 84–34 drubbing of Fairmont State College.

Cam Henderson, Marshall's legendary coach, described the new facility—a big change from cramped Radio Center—as "just about the answer to any coach's prayer. We have waited a long time for this but it was worth it."

Thus, the Field House seemed off to a great start. But there was trouble ahead.

Bonds issued by governmental bodies are of two types: general obligation bonds, which are to be repaid from future tax revenues, or revenue bonds, which are to be repaid from the dollars taken in by the enterprise the bonds financed. The two bond issues sold to finance the Field House were revenue bonds. The intent was that the bondholders would be paid with revenue generated by the rental fees the Field House charged those who booked events there.

Five months after the Field House opened, it seemed unlikely that the recreation board would be able to meet even the first bond payment of $15,000, which was due July 1, 1951. The board had been overly optimistic in its projections of how many events the Field House would book and how much revenue that would bring in. Simply put, the arena couldn't make its bond payments and still meet its payroll and other operating expenses. The first bond payment was made, but subsequent payments became more difficult. That meant the county and city had to step in and come to the building's rescue.

By 1956, the city and county were putting a combined $55,000 a year into subsidizing the Field House. (That may not seem like a great deal of money, but adjust the sum for inflation and it would be the equivalent of an annual outlay of more than $500,000 in 2017 dollars.) To resolve the financial problem, the city and county proposed a three-year tax levy that would completely pay off the bonds and leave the Field House free of debt. The voters approved the levy on May 8, 1956.

But that was by no means the end of financial troubles for the Field House. At the end of 1957, it no longer had to make bond payments but nevertheless was still running in the red because it wasn't taking in enough revenue to cover its payroll and other operating costs. In the fall of 1958, the management threatened to shut down the arena for a while due to a lack of operating funds.

And so it went over the years. It seemed the Field House always operated just a step ahead of bankruptcy. Bookings became even fewer in the 1980s, when Marshall built its own basketball court at Cam Henderson Center and the city opened the Huntington Civic Center (now the Big Sandy Superstore Arena).

The county was more than happy to turn the Field House over to the Cabell County Board of Education in 1986, and the school system was similarly relieved when it passed the building along to the Greater Huntington Park and Recreation District a decade later.

In 2011, the park district, faced with shelling out more than $1 million for a new roof, eagerly turned the Field House over to Marshall, which demolished it to make way for a new soccer complex.

NEWSPAPER BUILDING HAS STOOD TEST OF TIME

On May 21, 1923, Joseph Harvey Long celebrated his sixtieth birthday by turning the ceremonial first shovel of dirt for a new newspaper building that he vowed would be the most modern and complete in the state. Nearly a century later, Long's landmark building has stood the test of time. While much remodeled and expanded over the years, it's still home to the *Herald-Dispatch*.

A Pennsylvania native who had learned the printing trade in Wheeling, Long arrived in Huntington in 1893 with a meager bankroll and a big dream. On his arrival, Long purchased a fledgling newspaper, the *Huntington Herald*, paying $100 down and pledging to pay the balance of $1,700. He published the *Herald* for only eighteen months before selling it and purchasing another newspaper, the *Advertiser*.

Floyd S. Chapman, a future several-term mayor of Huntington, was the city editor of the *Advertiser* but later became editor of the *Herald*. In 1904, he left to begin his own newspaper, the *Dispatch*. In 1909, the *Herald* and the *Dispatch* merged to become the *Herald-Dispatch*.

That set the stage for a battle royal between the city's two rival newspapers, as Long's afternoon *Advertiser* slugged it out with the morning *Herald-Dispatch*. Each was determined to enlist more readers than the other.

At that time, the *Advertiser* was published in a small building located on the future Fourth Avenue site of the Keith-Albee Theater. But that was about to change.

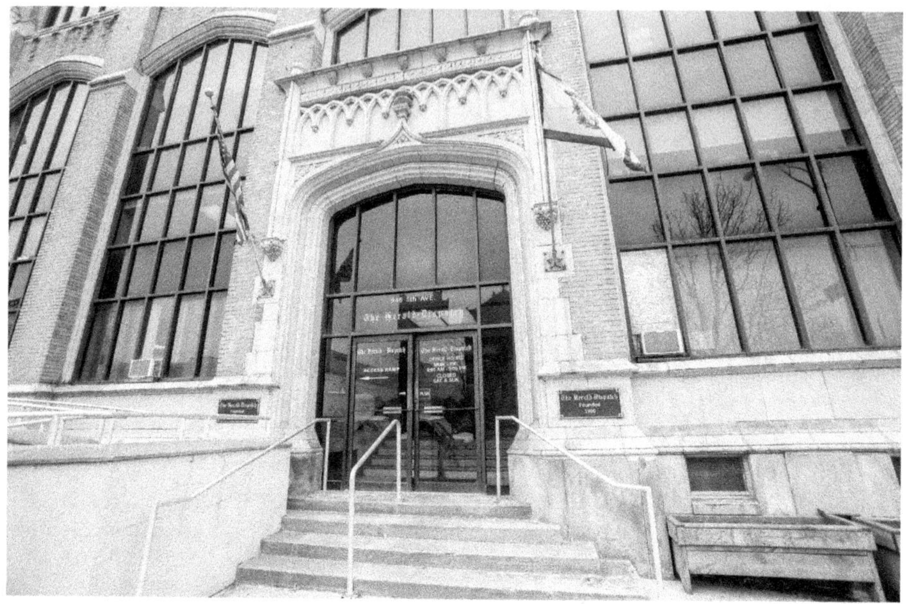

In 1924, J.H. Long finished construction of a building at Fifth Avenue and Tenth Street to house his newspaper, the *Advertiser*, but when it merged with the rival *Herald-Dispatch*, the building became home to both papers. *Herald-Dispatch*.

The Fifth Avenue Baptist Church was then located on the northwest corner of Fifth Avenue and Tenth Street, but the growing congregation needed a bigger building. In 1916, Long paid the Baptists $93,000 for their old church, and they set about erecting their present church at Fifth Avenue and Twelfth Street. Long had the church building demolished and hired two of the city's best-known architects, the father-son team of Robert Lum Day and Sidney Logan Day, to design the new building he envisioned.

Robert Day was born in Georgia in 1853. The Days were Unionists who refused to support the Confederacy. As a result, the family lost their jewelry business during the Civil War. Leaving the South, Robert worked as a surveyor for his uncle, Martin Lum, who was chief construction engineer for the Chesapeake & Ohio Railway. Settling in Huntington, Day went to work for the Ensign Manufacturing Company. In 1900, he began a contracting business, to which he added work as an architect. Some of his work included Catlettsburg (Kentucky) City Hall and the west wing of the Cabell County Courthouse. He and his wife, Mary Martha Johnson, had two children: a daughter, Florence, who died in infancy, and a son, Sidney. Robert retired in 1924 and died four years later.

Sidney Day was born in Huntington in 1887, graduated from Marshall College in 1906 and began working with his father. To further his education, he attended the Massachusetts Institute of Technology, graduating in 1912 with a bachelor's degree in architecture. He returned to Huntington in 1913 and rejoined his father's business. After his father retired, Sidney continued working as an architect. His work included many churches, businesses and residences in Huntington. Among them were the Foster Memorial Home, the Beverly Hills and Highlawn Presbyterian Churches, the Hite-Saunders and Emmons Schools and the *Advertiser* building. He died in 1968.

The papers of the two architects, including the original plans for the newspaper building, are housed in Special Collections at the Marshall Library. They were donated to Marshall by Sidney Day's daughter Mary Toneson and his granddaughter Barbara Toneson.

C. Harrison Smith, a prominent local contractor, was hired to erect the newspaper building. A Pennsylvania native, he graduated from Marshall College and, in 1914, entered the contracting business in Huntington. His many projects included an addition to Simms School and a dormitory at Huntington State Hospital.

In a page-one article on the groundbreaking for its new building, the *Advertiser* reported the structure would be "three stories above the ground and two below" and would be built from reinforced concrete faced with pressed brick, terra cotta and stone. The article put the cost of the building at $100,000, with another $100,000 to be spent on "modern printing equipment, furniture, mechanical equipment and other features." The building, the article said, would measure sixty-five feet wide on Fifth Avenue and extend for eighty feet along Tenth Street.

"The *Advertiser* hopes to have the building completed by September," the article said. That was to prove wishful thinking. Rather than taking four months, it would require nearly a year to complete the building and ready it for occupancy.

The building's design placed its entrance on Fifth Avenue. The printing press was located in the basement, part of which extended out beneath the sidewalk in front of the building. A subbasement was designed for the storage of newsprint. The other floors contained a variety of spaces, including a large room where the reporters and editors would work.

On July 8, the *Advertiser* published a half dozen photographs of the excavation dug for the new building—"a tedious, laborious preliminary"—and reported the contractor shortly would begin pouring the basement walls. At the same time, the newspaper offered a new completion date: January 1, 1924.

The building was back in the news on August 19, with the *Advertiser* reporting that concrete had been poured for the first floor. When completed, the article promised, the building "will present one of the most magnificent spectacles in this section of the country. Not only will it be the most modern newspaper plant in West Virginia, but it will also be one of the most architecturally beautiful buildings in this and adjacent states."

The August 27 newspaper reported that work had started on the second floor. An October 2 layout of photographs indicated that work was proceeding on the third floor. A December 2 story reported that work on the exterior was all but complete and plans were being made to move into the building "during the last days of February."

February came and went. So did March and April. Finally, on May 5, a page-one headline announced: "Moving Day for the *Advertiser*." With it, a photograph showed a typesetting Linotype machine being lowered from the second story of the newspaper's old building. The paper installed a new press and new stereotyping equipment in its new building, but everything else was moved from the paper's old quarters—in the space of but a few hours, from Saturday midnight to Monday morning.

Tom Jobe of the Independent Transfer Company, which moved the *Advertiser*, said he wanted to buy the first two papers that came off the new press Monday afternoon and backed up his request with a ten-dollar check. That was five dollars each for two five-cent papers. His request was granted.

As the press rolled on the *Advertiser*'s first edition in its new home, throngs of curious onlookers crowded the Tenth Street sidewalk, where they could view the busy press through the building's big plate-glass windows.

The *Advertiser*'s new, modern building was the talk of the town. Not to be outdone, Dave Gideon, publisher of the *Herald-Dispatch*, immediately built his paper a handsome new structure at 914 Fifth Avenue, next door to the old Cabell County Public Library and just a few doors down from the *Advertiser*. (The building now houses a law firm, Farrell, White & Legg, PLLC.)

The battle between the two rival newspapers raged for months and might have gone on longer, but peace negotiations were going on behind the scenes. On August 8, 1927, the newspapers' two publishers announced they had reached an agreement to pool their resources. A new firm, the Huntington Publishing Company, was formed with Long as chairman of the board and Gideon as president.

The *Herald-Dispatch* abandoned its building and moved into the *Advertiser*'s. The business and mechanical operations of the two papers were combined, although their news staffs remained separate. For the next decades, the old building's press published the *Advertiser* each afternoon, the *Herald-Dispatch* each morning and a combined edition, the *Herald-Advertiser*, on Sundays.

In 1957, the newspaper company purchased a new Wood Metropolitan press and installed it in the basement of a new addition constructed at the rear of the building. (Sadly, passersby no longer could look in and see the press whirling away.)

In 1971, the local owners of the Huntington Publishing Company newspapers sold them to Hawaii's *Honolulu Star-Bulletin*. Only months later, the Gannett Company, one of the nation's largest newspaper chains, purchased both the Honolulu newspaper and the Huntington papers. Gannett invested millions of dollars to modernize the Huntington papers, including the 1974 construction of another addition to the building, one that extended it to the rear alley.

In 1979, the *Advertiser*, like many other afternoon newspapers, discontinued publication, a victim of changing tastes on the part of readers who now much prefer morning newspapers. At the same time, the Sunday *Herald-Advertiser* nameplate was retired and the *Herald-Dispatch* became a seven-day-a-week publication. After the *Advertiser* folded, many of its longtime staffers moved to the *Herald-Dispatch*.

In 2007, Gannett sold the *Herald-Dispatch* to another national chain, GateHouse Media. A month later, GateHouse in turn sold the newspaper to Champion Industries, a commercial printer, business forms manufacturer and office products and furniture supplier headed by local businessman Marshall Reynolds.

In 2013, Champion Industries sold the *Herald-Dispatch* to HD Media Company, LLC, a company formed specifically for the purpose of buying the newspaper assets from Champion. Doug Reynolds, son of Marshall Reynolds, is the managing member of HD Media Company.

Thus, the *Herald-Dispatch* continues to operate in a historic building that was conceived and built by its great rival, Joseph Harvey Long, for his *Advertiser*.

OPENING OF PULLMAN SQUARE ENDED SUPERBLOCK SOAP OPERA

When Pullman Square was dedicated in 2004, it opened an exciting new chapter in the city's history—and wrote an end to a long-running local soap opera.

TV soap operas have more emotional ups and downs than an elevator. Their writers fill the scripts with dizzying highs and crushing lows for their make-believe characters. And it was that same sort of up-and-down melodrama that hung over Huntington's Superblock for more than thirty years.

In the 1960s and '70s, many cities across the nation embarked on urban renewal projects aimed at reshaping their downtowns. Huntington joined that trend in a big way. The Huntington Urban Renewal Authority acquired a big slice of the city's downtown and leveled much of it. Dozens of downtown businesses, both large and small, were forced to relocate. Some elected to close their doors instead.

The downtown makeover spawned a number of notable construction projects, including a new Cabell County Public Library, a new building for the First Huntington National Bank (today's J.P. Morgan Chase), a new Red Cross Center and Harris Riverfront Park, among others.

But most of a site envisioned as the centerpiece of the revamped downtown—four square blocks bounded by Eighth Street, the north side of Third Avenue, Tenth Street and Veterans Memorial Boulevard—would remain a weed-infested parking lot for decades, defying efforts to develop it.

Because of its size, the site became known as the "Superblock," but it quickly became clear the only thing super about it was its nine-acre size.

When the buildings on it were leveled in 1970, there was a dream about what might be built there. But that's all it was—a dream. There was nothing in the way of a master plan until 1974, and even then it was a plan that went nowhere.

The first company to step forward and try to develop the Superblock was Arlen Realty & Development of New York. Its $20 million concept was basically a traditional shopping mall. But its plan went sour when the company was unable to entice any anchor tenants for the proposed mall. In 1974, Arlen Realty was forced to file for bankruptcy.

In 1977, the Huntington Civic Center (today's Big Sandy Superstore Arena) was constructed on the western end of the Superblock, but that still left most of the tract vacant.

The next year, a group of local entrepreneurs offered a proposed $50 million development that included a 350-room hotel, retail stores, an office building and even a TV station. The plan remained under consideration for a couple of years but then was quietly abandoned.

In 1983, the National Shamrock Development and Investment Company took a one-year lease on the Superblock while it launched a search for

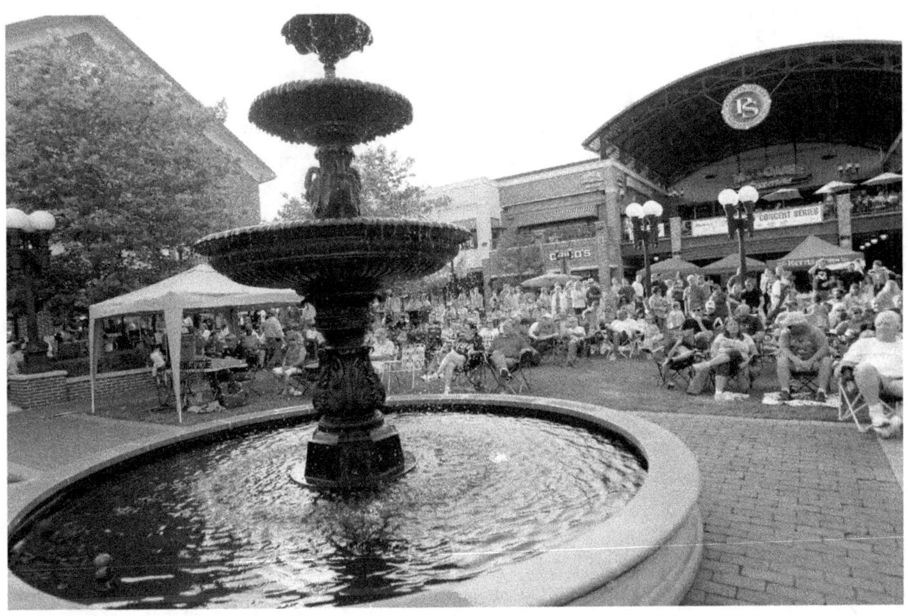

When the old buildings on downtown's Superblock were leveled, there was a dream about what might be built there, but it was decades before construction of Pullman Square made that dream a reality. *City of Huntington.*

possible tenants. The next year, Shamrock asked for a one-year renewal of its lease. At the end of the two years, the company indicated it was no longer interested in the property.

An off-track betting casino, christened Teletrack, was suggested for the site in 1986. Backers said they would model it on a Connecticut casino that had been erected in New Haven. The proposal sparked immediate controversy as local pro- and anti-gambling forces prepared to wage battle. Before the fight really got going, however, Governor Arch A. Moore Jr. vetoed an off-track betting bill that would have been necessary to legalize the venture.

In 1987, the Webb Companies, a development firm headquartered in Lexington, Kentucky, presented an ambitious plan for a Superblock project it dubbed RiverCenter. The $110 million plan proposed a twenty-story office tower atop a city-owned underground parking garage, along with a fountain, a reflecting pool and a skywalk leading over the floodwall and down into Harris Park.

Mayor Bobby Nelson was an enthusiastic backer of the RiverCenter plan, calling it a "beautiful, beautiful package." But ultimately, the Webb Companies threw in the towel when they couldn't sign the two major tenants they needed to make the office tower a reality.

Yet another proposal envisioned construction of an outlet mall on the property. The idea seemed popular with local shoppers but failed to materialize.

In 1998, a Holiday Inn was constructed adjacent to the Big Sandy Arena, between Eighth and Ninth Streets. However, much of the Superblock remained as vacant as ever.

Huntingtonians had seen their hopes dashed so many times before that, understandably, many people found it difficult to get excited when, in the late 1990s, Major Jean Dean, Tri-State Transit Authority general manager Vickie Shaffer and others began talking about a new development plan for the long-vacant property.

But this time the talk was very much real.

From the first, the vision for what became Pullman Square was that it would resemble an old-time small town and would fit within the historic context of the existing downtown Huntington. The hope was that the new retail/restaurant/entertainment complex would be a magnet, luring people back downtown, while sparking redevelopment elsewhere in the downtown—a hope that has been dramatically realized. Pullman Square indeed has written a long-overdue happy ending to the long-running Superblock soap opera.

INDEX

M

N

P

R

S

T

U

V

W

ABOUT THE AUTHOR

Over the years, amateur historian James E. Casto has researched and written countless newspaper and magazine articles exploring people, places and events in the history of Huntington, West Virginia. On the author's retirement from the *Herald-Dispatch* in 2004, Marshall University presented him with its John Marshall Medal of Civic Responsibility. In 2005, he was inducted into the Greater Huntington Wall of Fame. In 2006, the Cabell County Public Library named its James E. Casto Local History Room in his honor.